The Silk Road

To Lisa Diamond and Tim Duke

THE SILK ROAD

TAKING THE BUS TO PAKISTAN

Bill Porter

COUNTERPOINT

Library of Congress Cataloging-in-Publication Data
is available
ISBN 978-1-61902-710-7

Cover and interior design by Gopa & Ted2, Inc.
Typesetting by Tabitha Lahr

COUNTERPOINT
2560 Ninth Street, Suite 318
Berkeley, CA 94710
www.counterpointpress.com

Printed in the United States of America

Contents

The Silk Road

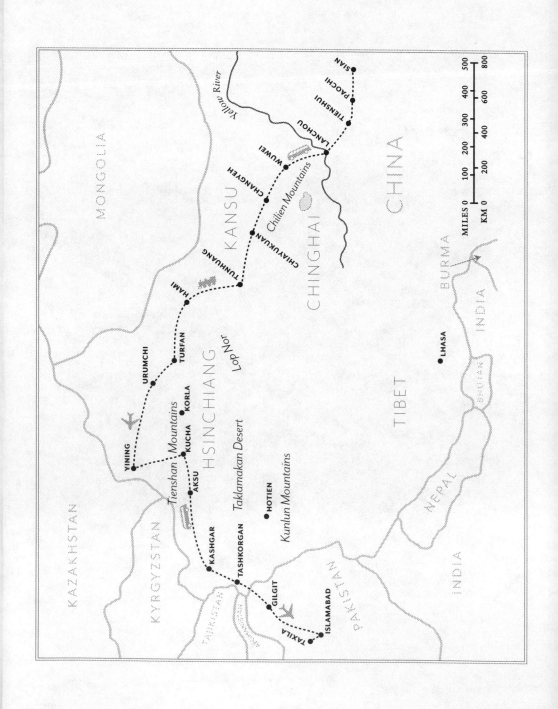

出發

1. Starting Out

E VER SINCE WE HUMANS FIRST BEGAN to walk, we have worn paths to our neighbor's house and to the next village and beyond. And ever since we discovered the wheel and learned to tame four-footed beasts, some of our trails have become roads. Among the more monumental examples are the hewn rock ramparts of ancient Rome's Appian Way and the poured concrete cloverleafs of the LA freeways. A much older, much longer, and at the same time less tangible example of our peripatetic nature is the Silk Road.

During its heyday, this will-o'-the-wisp highway carried bolts of silk from the Yangtze delta towns of Suchou and Hangchou across all of Asia to the shores of the Mediterranean, where it was exchanged for its weight in gold. But silk was only one of the road's important commodities. The Chinese spent just as much on incense and precious stones coming the other way. The road also brought many of the items still associated with China: musical instruments and forms of dance and art and religion—things we think of as integral to Chinese culture. For their part, the Chinese never called it the Silk Road. That honor goes to the nineteenth-century German scholar Baron Ferdinand von Richthofen—the uncle of Snoopy's nemesis, Manfred von Richthofen. The Chinese knew it only as the Road to the West. And traveling it was one of the most dangerous missions a person could undertake. It was a road through swirling sand and searing heat, past demons and apparitions, into lands that only the demented, exiled, or simply foolhardy dared venture. I wasn't sure to which category I belonged, but in the fall of 1992 I decided to travel this road, from China all the way to Pakistan. Because it was going to be a long and an arduous trip, I decided not to travel alone. I asked my friend Finn Wilcox to join me. Finn made his living planting trees and doing yard work. Fall was the beginning of his slack season, and so he signed on.

The Silk Road wasn't what a person would normally think of as a road. Until recently, there was no actual road, simply a trail of bones and animal dung left by the most recent caravan. A passing dust storm, and the road was gone, until the next caravan found its way across one of the world's more barren landscapes to the next oasis.

Exactly when or how this trade route developed, or who was responsible for its creation, remains a matter for archaeologists to work out. The migratory routes of nomads who lived in the grasslands of Central Asia crisscrossed this region, and certain groups stayed behind to settle low-lying pastures and oases. And when some found it more profitable to carry goods between these oases than herd their flocks, they provided the string that linked these islands of green together. But it wasn't until the time of Julius Caesar that this string turned to silk.

As I began to get ready, I considered what to take. Since I wasn't joining an organized tour that took care of baggage and transport problems, a suitcase was out of the question. And since I wasn't planning any sorties into the wilderness, so was a backpack. The problem with a backpack was that if the frame didn't break when someone threw something heavy on it, it got in the way trying to squeeze onto a bus or trying to work one's way down a train corridor. What I needed was a rucksack, in other words, a pack with shoulder straps but without a frame. And I just happened to have one. It was my old Forest Service rucksack. It repelled water and pickpockets, up to a point, and while it was only half as big as most backpacks, it held all that I needed.

First, I needed something to keep the whiskey in. Bottles were out of the question, and metal flasks weighed too much. I opted for a pint-size plastic bottle, one whose top screwed on securely. I couldn't afford to waste a drop. The Silk Road was littered with the bones of those who

Travelers' graves beyond Yangkuan Pass

couldn't make it to the next oasis. Once I had the pack and the whiskey out of the way, the rest was easy: a couple changes of clothes, long johns in case it turned cold, a cashmere vest for stepping out at night, and a lightweight jacket, a wool hat and gloves, just to make sure. And I never forget pictures of friends and family and earplugs and a flashlight and spare batteries and toilet paper. That was all I needed, that and a thermos. Finn's pack was pretty much the same.

Once we were packed, it was time to begin our big adventure. But where to begin? Since my plan was to travel westward as far as Pakistan, the most natural place to begin was at the Silk Road's eastern terminus in China. But it turns out that during the many dynasties that ruled China over the past few thousand years, the capital, and thus the eastern end of the Silk Road, varied. Sometimes it was in Loyang, and sometimes it was in Kaifeng. Sometimes it was even in Beijing. Usually, though, the road ended at the gates of Ch'ang-an, or Sian, as it's now known. So that was where we headed.

Since we were entering China from Hong Kong, we could have taken the weekly direct flight from the Crown Colony. But there was also a daily flight from Kuangchou, and flights from Kuangchou, being

domestic flights, were 50 percent cheaper. So we headed for Kuangchou. Unfortunately, the day we began our trip was August 29, which
turned out to be the beginning of Hong Kong's four-day Liberation
Day weekend, which celebrated Hong Kong's liberation from Japanese
occupation during World War II. Train tickets to Kuangchou had been
sold out for weeks, so we had no choice but to take the subway to Lo
Wu and walk across the border to Shenchen. Easier said than done.
Despite getting an early start, by the time we arrived at Lo Wu, half of
Hong Kong was in line. There we were just starting out, and already we
were beginning the weight-loss program that was part of every trip to
China. The temperature was in the nineties. We felt the ounces rolling
off as we shuffled slowly forward toward the oldest bureaucracy in the
world—which China introduced to the West, you guessed it, via the
Silk Road. Still, it was a bureaucracy that worked, and we finally made
it through immigration and customs. But when we came out the other
side, we found ourselves part of a mob. There were at least 10,000 people milling in front of the Shenchen train station. Like us, they were all
trying to get to Kuangchou.

We had tickets on the evening flight to Sian waiting for us at the
Kuangchou office of China Youth Travel Service. But we had to get
there before the office closed. We walked inside the station, but one
look at the lines sent us back outside, where taxis quoted their usual
absurd prices. After asking around, we got lucky, or so we thought. We
found a minivan bound for the city Westerners used to call Canton. It
was a brand-new minivan, too, and the fare was only 80RMB, or 80
Hong Kong dollars, take your pick. Since the RMB exchange rate at the
time was five to the US dollar, and the Hong Kong rate was eight, we
naturally paid in Hong Kong currency. We boarded, threw our bags up
by the driver and sat down. A few minutes later, four other passengers
boarded. Since the van was now full, the driver pulled out of the train
station parking lot. We were off. And out came the cards.

A man put his briefcase on his lap and laid out three cards faceup: the
three, the seven, and the queen of hearts. Then he turned them facedown
and moved them around and asked the other passengers to bet on the

location of the queen. The man who was running the game lifted up the edge of one of the cards so that Finn and I could see it. It was the queen. He said, "Come on. Here's your chance to make some easy money." Another player had already thrown down a thousand Hong Kong dollar bill on one of the other cards. It was the equivalent of 120 US dollars, and we could have used the money. It was going to be a long trip. But the hands of Lady Luck have usually turned out to be too slick for the likes of us, and our money stayed in our pockets.

The game continued without us, as two other passengers plunked down their money. We just smiled and watched, as did the other passengers. After a while, just as we reached the outskirts of Shenchen, the man running the game asked the driver to stop. He got off, as did the three "passengers" who had been betting. The only money in their pockets was the money they had when they got on. As we pulled away, everybody laughed.

In the border town of Shenchen, a fool and his money are soon parted. Apparently, the economic boom had attracted every crook and con artist around. If you're ever passing through Shenchen, keep that in mind. You might think you know where the queen is, but you can be sure the moment you put your money down, she'll turn up somewhere else.

Shenchen, though, wasn't quite finished with us. Not long after leaving the outskirts, our driver pulled over and announced he had engine trouble. He ordered us out and flagged down an old ramshackle regular-sized bus that was also headed for Kuangchou. He paid the bus driver one-fourth of what we had paid him, and we lumbered on in far less comfort thinking: "So long, Karl Marx. Hello, Groucho."

Still, at least we were lumbering, and four hours later we finally arrived in Kuangchou and picked up our plane tickets at the China Youth Travel Service office. As soon as the lid was lifted on China's service industry, travel organizations began popping up all over the place. Every province had its own, as did most major cities. Their prices were almost always lower than national organizations, like China Travel or China International Travel, but they weren't always easy to contact. Nor were they usually interested in anything less than a twelve-member group. During several previous trips, I had found China Youth Travel to be among the more reliable at the cheaper end of the spectrum. But times had changed.

In addition to asking them to arrange our plane tickets to Sian, I also asked if they could take care of the other arrangements on our itinerary, all the way to Islamabad. After checking with their Beijing office, China Youth's Hong Kong office told us it would cost us $4,000 apiece to see what we wanted to see. I may as well tell you right now it didn't cost half that for both of us. Still, China Youth Travel at least got us started with a couple of hard–to-get Liberation Day tickets to Sian, and our China Northwest Airlines flight left right on time. It reminded us, though, of the bus we had taken earlier from Shenchen—not the brand-new one, but the second, ramshackle one.

Before we took off, the stewardess walked down the aisle and handed out imitation sandalwood fans. At first we thought, "How nice, a gift." But we soon found out there was another reason behind the "gift." The pilot didn't turn on the plane's air-conditioning until after we were airborne. When the seat-belt light was finally turned off, one of the passengers walked up and looked at the thermometer attached to the plane's bulkhead. The temperature, he announced to all within earshot, was thirty-six degrees centigrade, or ninety-seven degrees Fahrenheit, and we weren't even on the Silk Road yet.

西安

2. Sian

A s our flight landed in Sian, the pilot turned off the plane's
air-conditioning, just as he did before we took off in Kuangchou.
Apparently, the plane's electrical system couldn't handle the load during
takeoff or landing. Two hundred imitation sandalwood fans all rose to
the occasion. At least we arrived.

The new Sian airport was farther out of town than the old one. It
was a forty-minute drive, and taxi drivers wanted 70RMB. We opted
for the airport bus, which was 5RMB and which left as soon as everyone collected their bags and climbed aboard. An hour later, we checked
into our hotel.

Since my first visit to Sian in 1989, a dozen high-end hotels had opened, but we chose the good old Victory. It was just outside the city's Hoping Gate, and a double without a bath was still only $8 a night. After dropping our bags in our cement-walled room, we walked back through the gate to Boss Wang's Three Star Restaurant. It was Boss Wang who'd kept me and Steve Johnson from being deported or imprisoned two years earlier. That was when Steve and I got caught inside a restricted area in the mountains south of town where the poet Wang Wei once lived but where nuclear warheads were now being manufactured. Boss Wang gained our release by entertaining the local foreign affairs police for two nights.

Wang and the Three Star were still going strong, and he feted us with all the cold beer we could drink. Wang said the police still stopped by to ask about Steve and me. I told him to say hello but suggested he not mention the book I had finally published based on my earlier trip. Somehow a photograph of the weapons factory's high-capacity heat sink got slipped in. Just before they'd arrested us coming down the mountain, we spotted them before they spotted us, and Steve put his exposed film in his socks and new film in his camera. It was our own version of the shell game. So where was the queen of hearts?

Finally, in a manner of speaking, we were on the Silk Road. In ancient times, Sian, or Ch'ang-an, as it was called, served as the capital during China's most glorious periods, the Han and the T'ang dynasties. In the city's new History Museum, visitors can see statues of foreign travelers who arrived during its heyday. The bearded merchants on whom those statues were based wouldn't have been hard to find. Ch'ang-an, after all, was the eastern terminus of the Silk Road. Still, unless they did so at imperial request, foreigners weren't allowed to spend the night inside the city. They could enter during the day, but they had to be outside the city's West Gate by nightfall. That was where deals were made, where foreign merchants bought their silk, and where they divested themselves of their own goods, including incense and colored glass from India, precious stones from Arabia, and medicinal plant and animal products from as far away as East Africa.

Nowadays, the area around the West Gate has been taken over by factories and apartment buildings, and the foreigners have moved to downtown hotels. Over the past decade, Sian has become a major stop on every foreigner's travel itinerary. After all, who visits China without seeing the Underground Army? Certainly, not us.

So the next morning, we boarded a local bus bound for the nearby town of Lintung and transferred to an even more local bus that took us the rest of the way to where the Terracotta Warriors were unearthed. The army was located in a huge single-story building that looked like an aircraft hangar. The price of admission for foreign visitors was $8, which made it the most expensive admission ticket in China. Not that it wasn't worth it, but that brings me to another subject: how to get in for less, a lot less. The solution is the old fake ID, which allows a foreign visitor to get in for the same price Chinese pay. The best ID's are those for students or teachers. Ours said we taught mechanical engineering at Sian's Northwest Engineering College. They cost us 100RMB apiece, and I reckon they saved us ten times that during our Silk Road trip alone. Not only could they be used for admission tickets, they could also be used for accommodations and even train tickets.

Of course, a fake ID is a fake ID; that is, it's illegal. Which brings up the question of breaking the law. I have always tried my best to respect the laws of countries through which I have traveled. But I make an exception in the case of laws or practices that discriminate against travelers by charging them double, triple, even ten times what locals pay for the same goods or services. My response to such discrimination is the fake ID. Naturally, I would never advise anyone to follow my example. But fake ID's are available wherever foreign travelers and local entrepreneurs meet. The cafes and hostels in Yangshuo and Dali, for example, do a booming business in this sort of discrimination equalizer.

Meanwhile, back to the Underground Army. When the ticket puncher wondered how we managed to buy tickets that were normally only issued to Chinese visitors, we just shrugged, said we were teachers, and walked through the big door and past the souvenir shop and suddenly found ourselves inside the building that enclosed the excavated pit. It was as big as a large cemetery. But in this case, the skeletons had been replaced by clay soldiers buried here more than two thousand years ago.

Their mission was to protect the eternal repose of the First Emperor, who, himself, was buried in 209 BC in a copper palace less than a kilometer to the west. The First Emperor was credited with establishing control for the first time over all of what we still call China. In fact, the name China was derived from his short-lived Ch'in dynasty. The soldiers of his guardian army were first discovered by farmers who were digging a well in 1974. Because the underground roofs had collapsed over time, their terracotta likenesses had been reduced to rubble. But more than a thousand of them had been carefully reconstructed and repositioned in their original battle formation. The result is one of the most impressive sights in China. Next to the Great Wall and the Forbidden City, this is the most visited sight in the Middle Kingdom, although not the most photographed. Visitors had to pay a special fee to take pictures, and guards were posted to make sure everyone complied. This restriction has since been changed, but at the time of our visit, our cameras stayed in our arm bags, and our arm bags had to be checked before we could enter.

As for the First Emperor's tomb, the one that the soldiers were guarding, it had yet to be excavated. Its contents were thought to be beyond the ability of the authorities to preserve. They had their hands full with the Underground Army, which they were still excavating during our visit. Impressive though it was, a person could only stare at such a sight for so long. After half an hour, we had seen enough. We retrieved our arm bags and headed back to the road to catch a shuttle back to Lintung and another bus back to Sian. While we were walking out to the road, we saw a sign behind the building that enclosed the Underground Army. It said, WE MAKE TERRACOTTA SOLDIERS USING SAME STYLE, SAME MATERIAL, SAME QUALITY, SAME VALUE. WE STAND ON THE ORIGINAL KILN OF 2,000 YEARS AGO. AND WE REPRODUCE ALL ITEMS USING SAME CLAY, SAME SKILL, SAME FACIAL FEATURES, SAME WONDER OF THE WORLD. It was another reminder that we were, after all, on the Silk Road, where everything was for sale, even wonders of the world.

Big Goose Pagoda

But we weren't done with wonders. Back in Sian we changed buses and went to see the sight that symbolized the city, the sight on every promotional brochure. In its ancient guise as Ch'ang-an, Sian was the biggest city in the ancient world. Between the sixth and ninth centuries, between one and two million people lived within its fifty-kilometer-long walls. Among those people was the monk, Hsuan-tsang. Over the centuries, Hsuan-tsang's travels have been elevated through invention and allegory into one of the most famous of all Chinese stories: *Journey to the West*, in which Hsuan-tsang appears as the monk Tripitaka. "Tripitaka" is the Sanskrit word for the Buddhist canon, and its application to Hsuan-tsang wasn't inappropriate. More than any other single traveler, it was he who brought back the sacred texts that comprised the Chinese version of the Tripitaka.

Against his own emperor's wishes, Hsuan-tsang set off for India at the beginning of the seventh century. When he returned twenty-five years later, the emperor went outside of the city to welcome him back personally. The route Hsuan-tsang chose was substantially the same one we planned to travel—though we hoped it wouldn't take us as long and we wouldn't be beset by as many demons and dangers. Just to make sure, we lit some incense at the base of the pagoda Hsuan-tsang built to house the collection of scriptures he brought back from India. It was called Big Goose Pagoda, and it was still there at the southeast corner of the city. In fact, it had been the symbol of the city ever since it was built in 652. While our sticks of incense were still burning, we climbed the steps that led to the top of the pagoda. A few minutes later, we finally reached the seventh and final story. There were open archways on all four sides. We stood at the one that looked west. The Silk Road began just beyond the rooftops.

出城

3. Leaving Town

AFTER PAYING OUR RESPECTS to one of the most famous Silk Road travelers, the only thing we needed was a bus. And that was easily arranged at the city's West Gate, where foreigners and Chinese have been setting off on the Silk Road for the past 2,000 years (although on camels and horses). After a night of hard drinking with Boss Wang, we found our ride waiting for us the next morning at the West Gate Bus Station, just as the sun was coming up. We added our packs to a pile

of other bags that covered the engine cowling next to the driver. And off we went, through Sian's West Gate and onto the Silk Road. A few kilometers later, we passed a Silk Road monument being constructed on the road's divider. It was made of huge blocks of pink granite and recreated an entire caravan: camels, bearded foreigners, and, of course, their merchandise. I wondered if a future monument would include a bus.

In any case, we were off, on the Silk Road at last, even if we were a bit shaky. The farewell banquet thrown for us by Boss Wang the night before was still with us. We tried to sleep, but we didn't sleep long. Ninety minutes after leaving Sian, the driver woke us just in time to let us off at the turnoff to Maoling, which was two kilometers to the north.

Several three-wheelers were waiting at the roadside, and we threw our gear into one and headed for the pile of dirt beneath which Emperor Wu of the Han dynasty was buried over 2,100 years ago, a hundred years after the First Emperor died. Over the course of fifty years, one-third of the government's annual revenue was spent on the tomb's construction. One can only imagine what treasures it contains. But even though it was built as far underground as possible, parts of it were looted sixty years later by a rebel army. From outside, it looked like the First Emperor's tomb: a grass-covered hill—a large hill, but just a hill. The only thing that suggested it might be more than that was a stone camel at the base that visitors could mount for a souvenir photo. Emperor Wu, more than any other man, was responsible for establishing Chinese control of the eastern half of the Silk Road. He saw plenty of camels in his day.

Emperor Wu ascended the dragon throne in 141 BC at the young age of sixteen, and he stayed on the throne for fifty-four years, longer than any other Chinese emperor. His reign marked one of the most glorious periods of the Chinese empire. It also marked the beginning of Chinese expansion along the Silk Road. In fact, one of Emperor Wu's first acts was to send an emissary to form an alliance with kingdoms along the Silk Road against the Hsiung-nu, or Huns, who were causing problems along China's northern and northwest borders. The emissary's name was Chang Ch'ien, and he left Ch'ang-an in 138 BC. Unfortunately, the

Grave mound of Emperor Wu

Huns found out about Chang's mission, and they captured him soon after he reached his first oasis.

Hoping to use him as a bargaining chip, they held Chang prisoner for ten years, until he managed to escape. Instead of returning home, Chang continued west and eventually returned to Ch'ang-an by another route. Although he failed to arrange any alliances with the enemies of the Huns, Chang brought back the first accurate account about the kingdoms that ruled the oases along the Silk Road.

Emperor Wu was intrigued, and he sent Chang back to establish ties with as many of the kingdoms as possible. This time Chang traveled about as far as we planned to travel, all the way to the fringes of the Persian Empire. Chang's second trip was a great success, and the information he brought back supplied the basis for a series of military campaigns that extended Chinese influence westward. Thus began the Great Game for control of Central Asia that is still going on.

It was Emperor Wu who was responsible for initiating the Chinese policy of controlling Central Asia by controlling the Silk Road. And the man Emperor Wu chose to put that policy into action wasn't far away. His name was Huo Ch'u-ping. He was the nephew of the emperor's favorite concubine, Lady Wei. Despite his youth, he was a brilliant commander and succeeded, where others had failed, in driving the Huns out of the Kansu Corridor that connected China with the rest of the Silk Road. The emperor followed up Huo's military success by extending the Great Wall to encompass all the oases in the Kansu Corridor as far as Tunhuang and thus established Chinese rule for the first time along the eastern portion of the Silk Road.

When Huo died at the young age of twenty-four, the emperor ordered him buried beneath a mound shaped to resemble a peak of the Chilien Mountains that bordered the Corridor. Huo's grave was a kilometer northeast of the emperor's own tomb, and it had clearly benefited from the government's renewed interest in reminding its citizens of China's longstanding influence in Central Asia. Politics aside, the grounds were made into a lovely park. And at the top of the grave mound there was a pavilion from which visitors could view dozens of other imperial grave mounds dotting the plain.

As for Huo's own grave mound, its most noteworthy feature was the series of fourteen stone carvings at the base. They were ancient, but they looked almost modern in design. Among the most famous was one of a horse trampling a bearded foreigner, which made us feel a bit uneasy. Finn and I weren't Huns, but we do get a little rowdy from time to time. Fortunately we have so far survived our Hunnish lapses.

Since we were still recovering from our latest such lapse, we tried to keep moving. It was better than standing still. We returned to the highway and caught another bus. This time our ride was briefer. Thirty minutes later, we got off again. This time we stopped to visit the tomb of Yang Kuei-fei. In Chinese, "kuei-fei" means "imperial concubine." If there ever was an imperial concubine, it was Yang Kuei-fei. She was, if you will, the Madonna of the T'ang dynasty. There were those who even claimed she nearly brought about the dynasty's collapse as a result of her romance with Emperor Hsuan-tsung (not to be confused with the monk, Hsuan-tsang).

The first time Hsuan-tsung saw the lovely Lady Yang, she was being helped ever so slowly out of the hot-spring baths just east of Ch'ang-an.

Horse trampling barbarian at the grave of Huo Ch'u-ping

Although she was the wife of another noble, the emperor arranged for her to divorce her husband and to become a Taoist nun, after which he had her installed in his own harem. Affairs at court were never the same. The emperor was in love. The morning audience with his officials came to an end, and late night soirees began.

Meanwhile, Yang Kuei-fei's cousin took over as head of the government, and the country went to ruin. Rebellions sprang up, and before long the rebels were approaching the East Gate of the capital itself. All too soon the party ended. The emperor and his entourage fled Ch'ang-an through the West Gate and along the same road we were traveling. When they reached the spot where we got off the bus, his generals said they would go no farther unless he got rid of his love interest. They blamed the country's sorry state on the emperor's infatuation with his concubine and his indulgence of her cousin, whom he had made prime minister. The emperor had no choice. Lady Yang's cousin was executed, and the lovely Lady Yang was strangled before they continued. The rebellion was eventually put down, and the emperor returned to Ch'ang-an the following year. But what a sad return it must have been. One of China's greatest poets, Pai Chu-yi, commemorated this tale in his epic poem "Everlasting Sorrow." Did the emperor pause at his former lover's tomb on his return? Or did he recall how they had knelt together on the hillside above the hot-spring baths where the two first met? It was the seventh night of the seventh moon, and beneath its light the emperor and his concubine vowed to be reborn as the Herdboy Star and the Weaving Maid Star, in the constellations Aquila and Lyra. The Chinese say these two still meet this night once a year on a bridge formed by magpies. If their vows came true, I wonder if Yang Kuei-fei still peels the emperor's grapes or if she dips them in poison.

Her tomb was at the side of the highway behind a small shrine hall and consisted of a small stone-covered mound. The stones were added afterwards to prevent the grave from disappearing. Yang Kuei-fei was considered the most beautiful woman in China, and after she was buried here, it was said that the soil of her grave mound took on a wonderful

Tomb of Yang Kuei-fei

fragrance. Women came from all over to collect it. They rubbed the soil on their faces to remove blemishes and to make their skin feel softer. Even if the effect was only psychological, so many women came for Lady Yang Powder, as they called it, the grave mound began to disappear. To keep the tomb from being worn away entirely, the authorities had it covered with stones, and the stones finally put an end to the disappearing grave mound of Yang Kuei-fei. Over the past 1,200 years, many other visitors stopped here, and the courtyard surrounding her tomb was lined with their poems and inscriptions and with weeping willows planted by her many admirers.

After our own reverie, Finn and I walked back out to the road and flagged down the next bus headed west. It was a great way to travel. No reservations needed. We even found seats. The road we were on led past fields of corn and wheat that covered the Wei River Plain, where the soil is said to be a hundred meters deep in places—a mixture of river alluvium and windblown loess. Over the centuries it supported a dozen dynasties, beginning with the Chou.

This area west of Sian was once known as Chouyuan, the Plain of Chou. It was the ancestral home of the clan that founded the Chou dynasty around 1100 BC, the same dynasty whose rulers Confucius and Lao-tzu served six hundred years later. In addition to introducing major changes in government and society, the Chou was also famous for its bronzes. And archaeologists have found more bronze artifacts on the Plain of Chou than anywhere else in China. The reason isn't hard to find. The Silk Road went right through the Chouyuan Plain and provided a regular supply of tin. Tin is a key ingredient in bronze, and it arrived from as far away as what is now Ukraine.

In addition to thousands of bronzes, the Chouyuan Plain also yielded another important artifact, one with religious as well as historical significance. Three hours and 150 kilometers west of Sian, just north of the town of Fufeng, we asked the driver to let us off at Famen Temple, the home of the Buddha's finger bone. The bone was apparently brought to China via the Silk Road over 2,200 years ago at the behest of India's King Ashoka. After conquering most of the subcontinent, Ashoka was converted to Buddhism. And to propagate his new faith, he ordered the Buddha's remains to be distributed throughout the known world.

And so the Buddha's finger bone arrived in China in the third century BC. There was, however, no mention of this event. The reason, I'm guessing, is that the nature of the religion or its founder wasn't sufficiently understood to deserve mention. But the Chou rulers were at least hospitable enough to grant the embassy from India a burial plot in their royal burial ground north of Fufeng. It wasn't until much later, not until Buddhism arrived in China and Chinese monks returned from India, that they realized the treasure that had been bestowed upon them.

Thus, the earliest mention of the finger bone wasn't until the sixth century, when the ruler of the Northern Wei dynasty came here to pay his respects. Later, during the T'ang, the finger bone was reinterred in a series of gold coffins, and a huge pagoda was built over the site. Thus, Famen Temple came into being. Several years before our visit, when the pagoda was being rebuilt, its treasures came to light for the first time since the T'ang, and the finger bone was placed on display in a crypt at the base of the new pagoda. For a nominal fee, Finn and I even got a certificate proving that we did, indeed, pay our respects to the same finger that pointed to the Middle Path 2,500 years ago.

The finger bone, we noticed, was pointing west, which we took as a sign to return to the road. Once again, a bus was not hard to come by, and a few minutes later we were rolling westward again—but, once again, not for long. We got off thirty minutes later in the next town, Chihshan, and hired a three-wheeler to take us to the shrine of the Duke of Chou. The shrine is located eight kilometers to the north in the ancestral home of the two kings who founded the Chou dynasty 3,100 years ago. Following their deaths, the Duke took over the government until the next king was old enough to rule. It was under his guidance that the Chou instituted the administrative and ritual measures by means of which it was able to maintain its rule for 800 years. The Duke has been admired ever since as the perfect regent. Confucius went even further

Famen Temple Pagoda containing Buddha's finger bone

Roof ornamentation at Duke of Chou Shrine

and put the Duke on a par with the ancient sage kings of China's myth-
ological past. But then, Confucius had more reason to hold the Duke in
high regard. The ruler of the state of Lu, in which Confucius lived, was
himself the Duke's lineal descendant. And all the important rituals in the
state of Lu included obeisance to the ruler's noble ancestor.

Meanwhile, north of Chihshan, the Duke had a palace built for one
of his wives. Several verses of the *Book of Poems* edited by Confucius
even recall the setting. Ever since the Duke's death 3,000 years ago, his
memory has been honored here in one form or another. A pair of huge
locust trees planted 2,000 years ago still flourish. And the shrine hall's
spectacular roof ornamentation dates back 1,200 years to the T'ang.
But according to the shrine's present curator, these were nothing compared to what was planned in the hills behind the shrine: a reservoir
where visitors could water-ski.

That was enough to puncture our history balloon. Besides, it was
time to find a place to spend the night. We returned by three-wheeler to
the main highway and flagged down the next bus heading west. Just as

the sun was going down, our bus lurched into the town of Paochi, but not quite all the way. At the edge of town, a group of police stopped the bus to check tickets. Ooops! Not everyone had a ticket. In Communist China of old, where everyone was equal, although some were more equal than others, no one cared if anyone bought a ticket. But in the new Communist China with Socialist Characteristics, someone cared. The police dragged fifteen people off the bus, suggesting that word hadn't gotten around to everyone that they had to pull their own weight now, or at least buy a ticket.

By the time the bus finally arrived at the bus station there were only six of us left, and the sun was gone too. It had been a big day, and we didn't feel like spending any more time than necessary in finding a place to stay. From the bus station parking lot, we saw the rooftop sign of the Paochi Hotel beckoning two blocks away. And that was where we spent our first night on the Silk Road: at the Paochi Hotel, where our fake IDs got us a double with a bath for $8. A hot bath was never a bad thing. But I noticed that I was already feeling the first signs of the bronchial infection that often accompanied my trips to China. Why a bronchial infection? Because, when a billion people cleared their upper respiratory systems at regular intervals, in public, it was only a matter of time before the wind picked up the residue and deposited it in my lungs. Unfortunately, I had neglected to bring antibiotics. And so I spent my first night on the Silk Road with a slight fever. Still, at least I had a hot bath.

The next morning the fever had subsided, or at least it didn't keep me in bed. We went to visit the sights, of which Paochi had a few. In fact, one of China's oldest neolithic villages is inside the city: Peishouling, and it dates back 7,000 years. But we were more interested in the Taoist temple on the hillside behind the train station.

Named Chintai Temple, it was built in the fourteenth century. Before it was a temple, it was the residence of the Taoist master Chang San-feng, who lived here in the thirteenth century. According to local records, Chang was a most peculiar resident. Sometimes he went for months without eating. And sometimes he sat without blinking for ten

Chintai Temple and former home of Chang San-feng

days straight. And when he moved, he could travel 500 kilometers in a single day. And when he ate, he ate everything in sight.

Chang San-feng was a most peculiar man, indeed. And his only possessions were a straw hat and a robe of rags. But even the emperor was solicitous of his health—and not without reason. Chang San-feng was the greatest nei-kung master who ever lived. Some say he invented nei-kung, or internal kung-fu. Be that as it may, one day when he was sitting in his cave that overlooked the town's wooden houses and mud roads, he told one of his disciples to prepare his coffin, and he died the next day. But then, just as the coffin was being lowered into the grave, Chang came back to life, climbed out of the coffin, said good-bye to Paochi, and proceeded to Wutangshan in Hupei province. Over the succeeding centuries, Wutangshan became China's great kung-fu center, and whenever kung-fu contests were held, the Taoist monks of Wutangshan invariably came out on top. And it's said that Chang still appears there from time to time.

His former residence in Paochi was being restored. The caves that were carved into the loess cliff behind the temple where Chang and his disciples once lived had a new coat of whitewash and new rock archways. But apparently not many people cared. The archways were already covered by a jungle of chartreuse morning glories.

From the terrace in front of Chang's former home, we looked out across the Panhsi River to the north. Fifteen kilometers north of Paochi, where the Panhsi flowed into the Wei was where another early Taoist used to fish. His name was Chiang Tzu-ya, and one day over 3,000 years ago, Emperor Wen of the state of Chou was riding by and noticed there was something peculiar about the way Chiang was fishing. He stopped and discovered that Chiang was fishing without a hook. That was just the sort of man Emperor Wen was looking for, and Chiang became Emperor Wen's teacher as well as the teacher of the next two emperors, who together founded the Chou dynasty. The boulder on which Chiang Tzu-ya fished was said to still be there, as well as the shrine first built in his honor in the T'ang.

That was the view to the north. To the south, we could see a road winding into the serrated ridges of the Chungnan Mountains and beyond them into the Chinling Range. The road led through the Sankuan Pass and eventually into Szechuan. That was the same road Lao-tzu took when he disappeared 2,500 years ago after writing his famous treatise on the Tao known as the *Taoteching*. After Lao-tzu left Paochi, he was never heard from again, though some say he continued on to India. In ancient times, there was a road to India from Szechuan through Yunnan and Burma, but it was incredibly dangerous, and hardly the sort of road for a man who preached the doctrine of effortlessness. It certainly was not the sort of road for me and Finn.

We returned to the hotel, grabbed our bags, and walked to the train station, where we waited for the next train heading west. We were going farther this time than the local buses were going. As usual, the only tickets for sale were for standing room. But there was something new about the station. It had a "no smoking, no spitting allowed" waiting room. If that wasn't enough of a surprise, there was more. The next train heading west not only pulled in on time, it was half empty, and we stretched out with four seats for the two of us.

On our way out of the train yard, we waved to a couple of hobos doing the same thing as us but on a flatcar. Paochi was a major switching yard for freight trains, and we wondered if Chinese hobos were like American hobos, like Crummy Willy, for example—a hobo Finn met one day in Portland, Oregon.

As Finn tells it in his book *Here Among the Sacrificed*:

> *Willy pours the beans from his can into ours, and while we fill our empty bellies, he chuckles about the fine free lives we're living. "Damn me, if that wasn't the slowest ride I ever had. And that kid? Something wrong with him. Kept offering him food, but he wouldn't eat it. Said it's no good for you, too much of this or that in it. But what the hell, I told him. You got to eat whatever you can get. I think he escaped from some kind of nuthouse."*
>
> *Willy shakes his head and scratches at his foot by the firelight. "And he didn't want to drink or smoke. I think*

he was a little touched. But I told that crazy kid there's two things in my life I've never missed. A meal is one, and a frieght train is the other. Now, I'm not saying I haven't put that meal off a day or two. And them trains left more than once when I wasn't ready. But I haven't missed either of them yet." Willy climbs under his dirty blanket grinning, tickled with his little joke. "Well, it's time for this old hobo to get some sleep. Going to be another big day tomorrow. Good night, fellas." Good night, Crummy Willy.

But it was early morning and not night. Like hobos around the world, the ones we saw in the Paochi were probably looking for work and couldn't afford the bus or train fare to the next job. In America the first hobos were farmers with no land to farm, and they carried their hoes with them when they rode the freights. So people called them "hoe-boys." And eventually that got shortened to "hobos." And they were riding the freights in China too. As we pulled out of Paochi, we waved, and they waved back.

天水

4. Tienshui

ONCE THE TRAIN WAS UNDERWAY, it followed the Wei upstream through a series of gorges the river had cut through granite and loess and part the occasional terraced field of wheat or corn. With four seats to stretch out in, we had no trouble falling asleep. We were still recovering from our Sian getaway, and I was still feeling a bit feverish. So sleep was good. Three hours later, we got off in Tienshui. We were in Kansu province now. Sian may have been where the Silk Road began in China, but Tienshui felt like the beginning.

Upper reaches of the Wei River

In ancient times Tienshui was called Chinchou. It was the ancestral fief of the First Emperor, the man who founded the Ch'in dynasty. Until the Ch'in, Chinchou marked the limit of Chinese control of the Silk Road. Even in later dynasties to travel beyond Chinchou was to tempt fate. Those who could afford the cost, paid to have buddha statues carved into the cliffs nearby just to make sure they were paid up in Heaven. The cliffs where they chose to do this were sixty kilometers southeast of town, and outside the train station were a handful of minivans waiting to take people there. It was just past noon, and we figured we still had enough time to see the caves and get back to town before dark. We climbed aboard one of the minivans, and ninety minutes later our driver dropped us off at the foot of a very peculiar looking mountain. It was sheer on three sides, and from one angle it looked like a stack of wheat. In fact, that is what the Chinese called it: Maichishan, or Wheat Stack Mountain.

Wheat Stack was made of red conglomerate, which weathers rather easily. It also carves rather easily, and more than 1,600 years ago Buddhists began carving caves and niches into its cliffs and filling them with religious art. Tienshui was the first truly Chinese town travelers from the West entered. After traveling for months on the caravan routes, Tienshui must have seemed like paradise. The area was known for its forests and lakes and rivers. Buddhism flourished here early, as merchants and travelers alike paid to have images carved on Maichishan to thank the gods for their safe arrival.

The earliest statues date back to the late fourth century, and the earliest communities of monks and nuns to the early fifth. Among the nuns was the wife of the Chinese emperor. Her name was Lady Yi-fu, and she was renowned for her virtue and patronage of her adopted religion. The emperor could have cared less. To cement relations with a nomadic tribe on his northern border, the emperor added another wife to his harem and ordered his first wife to shave her head and become a nun. Lady Yi-fu obliged and moved to Maichishan. But the emperor's new wife was still suspicious, and she prevailed upon the emperor to order Lady Yi-fu to commit suicide. Again, she obliged. Traces of her tomb are still visible in cave forty-three, only one of the mountain's nearly two hundred caves.

Maichishan isn't really a mountain. It's a big monolith of red rock sticking out of the foothills of the Chinling Mountains. But the caves are real, all 194 of them. And they're filled with statues of buddhas and bodhisattvas and heavenly deities. The basic method of construction was to drive a set of wooden posts into the rock then mold the figure of a buddha or bodhisattva onto the posts. This was the early days of Buddhism in China, and apparently it was a time when the buddhas were still allowed to smile. But the real surprise at Maichishan wasn't the smiling buddhas. The real surprise was the murals on the walls behind the figures. Every niche had its own set of colors and its own array of painted flowers—even its own view of paradise. The only drawback was that unless visitors hired their own guide at the reception center, they had to limit themselves to whatever they could see through the gates and grills and the bars and wire mesh—except, of course, for those statues too big to put in a cave. Finn and I decided to set off on our own. Since most of Maichishan's caves and statues stretch across the sunny, southern half of the mountain, we worked our way up the various levels of scaffolding there and looked inside dozens of caves that visitors without a guide could still access. In the past, people must have prayed a lot on their way up and down the old wooden scaffolding. Nowadays, things were easier. Now visitors prayed on their way up and down the new steel scaffolding. Finn and I prayed too. We felt like high-rise window washers.

After an hour or so of this, we felt exhausted by the inherent stress of such sightseeing. We made our way down the mountain and returned to Tienshui by minivan just as the sun was going down. Despite the presence of Maichishan in the area, Tienshui didn't have much in the way of tourist facilities. None of the hotels near the train station had hot water, and we wanted a bath. Everyone agreed: the only hotel with hot water was the fancy Tienshui Guesthouse twenty kilometers west of town. What the hell. We jumped in yet another minivan, and thirty minutes later checked in. At least we had a room and hot water. Although it was

Finn and author at Maichishan

too dark to see, the hotel clerk said from our room there was a view of Mount Wenshan where Li Kuang was buried.

Along with Huo Ch'u-ping, whose tomb we had already visited, Li Kuang was instrumental in ridding the Silk Road of the Huns and bringing it under Chinese control. The Huns called Li "The Flying General," and they avoided him like the plague. Once, when Li was far from his main force with only a hundred men, he was surprised by a Hun force of several thousand cavalry. Despite the overwhelming odds, the Huns refused to attack, suspecting it was just another of Li's traps. On another occasion, the Huns wounded and captured Li. They put him on a litter and rode off to show their prize to the Great Khan. But when the other riders got a little too far ahead, Li overpowered one of his captors, grabbed his bow and arrows and rode off on the man's horse. Several hundred Huns gave chase, but they soon turned back when Li started dropping them one by one with his deadly bowmanship.

Although Li was feared by the Huns, he was not popular at court and was forced into premature retirement on several occasions by others jealous of his exploits. But whenever Li left Kansu, the Huns returned in force. And sooner or later, the emperor had no choice but to order him back into action. Even when Li was an old man, he was still fighting the Huns. And he fought them until he lost his way in the desert one day and failed to rendezvous with another Chinese force led by the emperor's nephew. When the nephew sent his chief aide to reprimand Li, Li said to his officers, "Ever since I was old enough to wear my hair in a topknot, I've fought the Huns. I've fought over seventy battles and never lost. But now I've lost my way. It must be the will of Heaven. I'm over sixty and too old to endure such disrespect from some petty aide." He then drew his sword and cut his own throat. The Han dynasty historian Ssu-ma Ch'ien says that when Li died, the people of the empire—whether they had known him or not—were moved to tears, so deeply were they touched by Li's sincerity. No one knows for sure where Li's body ended up, but his uniform and the sword with which he cut his throat were buried there on Wenshan, just outside our window at the Tienshui Guesthouse.

When we were finally able to see the mountain the next morning, it looked farther away than we felt like hiking. We decided to limit our-selves to a respectful nod in Li Kuang's direction. There was a minivan waiting outside the hotel, and thirty minutes later it dropped us off at an easier place to visit than Li's grave. It was a shrine to Fu Hsi. Fu Hsi lived 5,000 years ago and was the first of China's sage emperors. Although most of his exploits were associated with the Yellow River plains, Tienshui was his ancestral home. His name means "tamer of animals" in Chinese, and he was reportedly the man who led the early Chinese from the hunting–gathering stage to the farming stage based on animal husbandry.

The taming of animals was only one of Fu Hsi's achievements. He was also a thinker and was credited with inventing one of the most basic concepts of Chinese philosophy, the division of all phenomena as belonging to the categories of Heaven, earth, and humanity and of all processes as being either yin or yang—that is, characterized by decrease or increase. Since the possible permutations of three levels of any duality are eight in number, Fu Hsi drew eight diagrams, with straight, heavenly lines for yang and broken, earthly lines for yin. Thus was born the *Yiching*, or *Book of Changes*, near Tienshui's West Gate, where we paid our respects before joining the next caravan out of town.

蘭州

5. Lanchou

T HE NEXT CARAVAN WAS THE MORNING express to Lanchou. The
   previous night we had to go twenty kilometers west of Tienshui to
find a hotel with hot water. The next morning, when we arrived at the
train station, instead of the usual assortment of noodle stands, we were
greeted by a half a dozen old ladies who had set up basins on the train
station steps, and they were waiting for us with towels and thermoses
of hot water. It was a wonderful experience, washing our faces in the
morning sun before boarding the Silk Road express.

It was a good thing we began the day feeling so clean. When our train finally arrived, and we began walking down the corridors looking for seats, it was like walking through one of the lower levels of Hell. It was as if the passengers had spent their whole lives there, as if they had been born there and some had died there and their bodies had been cannibalized and their bones scattered on the floor, waiting only to be swept out to fertilize the vineyards and melon fields that had now replaced the corn and wheat.

One by one, we worked our way through the cars, until finally we reached the sanctuary of the dining car. The bronchial infection that had been dogging me for several days had upgraded its status, and I now had a fever. The empty seats and tables of the dining car beckoned like an oasis. But just as we stepped inside, the conductor chased us back out. It wasn't mealtime. And so we retreated with our packs to the relatively unobstructed space between two cars. And for the next seven hours, that was where we stayed: between the boiler room with its attendant pile of coal and the toilet that train personnel kept locked for their own use. Fortunately, the beer cart came through at least once an hour, and when no one was looking the toilet door yielded to the magic of my needle-nose pliers. Yes, needle-nose pliers, one more item you'll want to bring with you on the Silk Road.

Finally, in the late afternoon the train pulled into Lanchou, and we were able to put an end to our misery. Lanchou hugs both banks of the Yellow River for more than twenty kilometers. After Sian it's the biggest city on the Silk Road, a position of which it is immensely proud. Like Sian, Lanchou also had a new, block-long pink granite sculpture of a camel caravan. The week we arrived, the city was even preparing for its first Silk Road Festival. Dignitaries were due to arrive from all over Northwest China. All we wanted to do was leave. Next to the train station, we checked at the long-distance bus station and bought tickets to our next destination, which was Wuwei. The bus wasn't leaving until around ten the next day, and since both of us were tired, and I wasn't feeling well, we proceeded to the Friendship Hotel and ended the day

Finn seated in poet-class

with a dinner I don't remember and a few beers I do.

Lanchou's position as a major way station on the Silk Road was never as great as it would like visitors to believe. When Marco Polo visited in the thirteenth century, he didn't find anything worth writing about. That was because in ancient times most caravans crossed the Yellow River at Hungshanhsia, a hundred kilometers east of Lanchou. That was where our old friend Emperor Wu crossed the river on his inspection tour of China's newly conquered northwest territory during the Han dynasty. Or if caravans didn't cross at Hungshanhsia, they chose another spot seventy kilometers to the west at a place called Pingling. Pingling was an especially popular place to cross the Yellow River in the T'ang, and the caves carved out of the nearby cliffs became one of China's great centers of religious art. It still boasts some of China's finest sculptures, but I had already visited the caves during my journey up the Yellow River, and I had a fever.

If I had felt better, we might have visited Linhsia, which was east of the Liuchiahsia Reservoir. The Linhsia area was one of the oldest known places of human settlement in China, and until modern times Linhsia, or Hochou as it used to be called, was a much more important stop on the Silk Road than Lanchou. Just outside Linhsia, archaeologists discovered a 5,000-year-old village, and among its remains they unearthed the earliest known bronze artifact found in China as well as the world's earliest known buds of cultivated hemp, or *cannabis sativa*. According to paleobotanists, the early ancestors of the Chinese used hemp as a textile fiber as well as a euphoric. And the nomadic tribes who served as intermediaries along the Neolithic version of the Silk Road carried the hemp from Linhsia to the Indian subcontinent, from which it eventually found its way to Africa and more recently to the Americas. In exchange for getting them high on hemp, the Indians reciprocated and sent the Chinese the hallucinogenic *datura*, a relative of the poisonous nightshade family that I saw growing wild when I visited the Linhsia area on my way up the Yellow River.

As a major way station on the Silk Road as far back as those Neolithic days, Linhsia had also seen many changes in its ethnic character.

Among those who had settled there in large numbers over the past thousand years were such Muslim groups as the Paoan, the Tunghsiang, the Salar, and the Hui. They all had stories to tell about how they ended up there, but the Tunghsiang tale was especially interesting.

According to an analysis of the Tunghsiang language and oral traditions, the Tunghsiang were a branch of the Sogdians and their ancestors lived in the region of Samarkand in what is now Uzbekistan or more than 3,000 kilometers west of Linhsia. Back at the beginning of the thirteenth century, the ancestors of the Tunghsiang became mercenaries in the army of Genghis Khan, and they followed the Great Khan to the Kansu Corridor—which just happened to be the scene of Genghis's final campaign. Genghis died in 1227 AD, east of Lanchou, and it wasn't until three years later that the Mongols consolidated their forces again and resumed a large-scale campaign against the Chinese. In the meantime, the Tunghsiang mercenaries took a liking to the Linhsia area. Linhsia, after all, had been visited by Muslim missionaries soon after the death of Muhammad, and the Islamic Tunghsiang felt at home there. They've been there ever since. At last count there were 38,000 Tunghsiang living in and around Linhsia, and over the centuries they've been joined by other Muslim groups, like the Salar, the Paoan, and the Hui.

Linhsia is also the area where much of the painted pottery in the Kansu Provincial Museum was unearthed, and until about a thousand years ago, Linhsia, and not Lanchou, was the major focus of Silk Road trade in this part of China. The old route was now somewhere beneath the Liuchiahsia Reservoir. But we were in Lanchou and the provincial museum was right across the street from our hotel.

We entered the next morning just as the guard opened the doors at eight o'clock. We had a ten o'clock bus to catch and asked the guard if we could leave our rucksacks with him, to which he agreed. Once we had divested ourselves of our bags, we headed straight for the painted pottery that dated back to China's Neolithic period 5,000 years ago. The pottery was first discovered in 1922 by the Swedish archaeologist J.G. Anderson following his earlier discoveries in the neighboring provinces of Shensi and Honan. The Kansu pottery, though, was more important because it constituted the earliest known representational art in China. The pots were meant to accompany the dead and were covered with red and black designs that looked like they were inspired by the swirling waters of the nearby Yellow River. The pots were huge, and there were dozens of them, each with a slightly different design. They were meant to hold water and grain for use in the afterlife. We lingered over them longer than we should have. They were so simple and yet so beautiful. But there was more that we wanted to see.

In addition to its world-class collection of Neolithic pottery, the museum also housed an excellent collection of bronzes, the most famous of which was the Han dynasty bronze horse unearthed in Wuwei. The artist added a wisp of cloud above the horse's head and placed one of its hooves on the back of a swallow to give it a feeling of movement. Since its discovery, the Flying Horse, as it was now called, had become the symbol of the Silk Road itself—which reminded us that our bus to Wuwei, where the Flying Horse was discovered, was leaving in an hour.

We retrieved our rucksacks from the guard and flagged down the first taxi we saw. Other than the museum, there really wasn't much else we wanted to see. I suppose if we had taken a later bus, we might have visited one of the city's two parks. But there wasn't a later bus. So we didn't visit Five Spring Park at the south edge of town where our young friend General Huo Ch'u-ping arrived in 121 BC. We had visited his tomb just after leaving Sian, but we had to pass up the place where he drew his sword in anger when he discovered there wasn't any decent water for his troops. Where he struck, water gushed forth. Five times he struck the ground, and five times water appeared. And his soldiers quenched their thirst and marched on to defeat the Huns. The springs have continued to flow and now supply the water for Lanchou's Five Spring Beer.

But we didn't have time to visit Five Spring Park, or the city's equally famous White Pagoda Park. The pagoda houses the remains of a Tibetan lama who died there in the thirteenth century. What made a visit to White Pagoda Park worthwhile wasn't so much the pagoda as the view from the hill on which it stood. From the photos we had seen, the pagoda looked down across the tiled roofs of the adjacent shrine

Lanchou's Yellow River Bridge

and the steel spans of the first bridge ever built across the Yellow River and on the swirling brown ribbon of the river itself. But it turned out we didn't have to visit White Pagoda Park to enjoy the view. Our bus crossed the same bridge and climbed the same hill behind the pagoda. From our bus windows, we looked down across the tiled roofs of the shrine below the pagoda and the bridge's steel spans and the swirling brown ribbon of water of the Yellow River, and we left Lanchou as we had found it, like a patient etherized upon a table.

6. Wuwei

A ND SO WE BEGAN OUR TRIP INTO the painted hills of the Kansu Corridor. On a map, Kansu looks like a bone, with its two joints at either end of a very long and very wide valley bounded by mountains to the west and deserts to the east. The Corridor is more than five hundred kilometers in length and at its narrowest only sixty kilometers wide. This is the section of the Silk Road the Chinese tried to control during the Han dynasty, and they established a number of garrisons.

One of the smaller garrisons was that of Lichien. The Silk Road is a most unusual road, and you never know who is going to show up on it next. The story involving Lichien began in 53 BC, when an army of Romans led by Crassus met the forces of the nomadic Parthians at a place called Carrhae in northern Iran. The Romans had never faced a skilled cavalry force before, and they were decimated. Over 20,000 Romans were killed, Crassus among them, and 10,000 Romans were taken prisoner.

Seventeen years later, in 36 BC, a Chinese army fighting near the western end of the Silk Road defeated a Hun force in what is now Uzbekistan, and among the prisoners they took were 145 Romans. They were survivors of the battle of Carrhae. Being professional soldiers, the Romans had no trouble disavowing their allegiance to the Huns and agreeing to fight for the Chinese, and they accompanied the Chinese army all the way back to the Kansu Corridor where they ended their days defending the garrison of Lichien. Lichien was long gone. But not far away was the first garrison established by the Chinese. It was the town of Wuwei, and after a five-hour bus ride from Lanchou that is where we arrived. It was a pleasant enough ride through rolling red hills and brown valleys, and the road was good. But the weather turned cold and rainy. By the time we arrived we had half our wardrobe wrapped around us.

As we pulled into town, Wuwei looked like a Silk Road city: flat and dusty. But unlike other Silk Road cities, Wuwei is Chinese, and it had preserved the typical military layout of a garrison town. Wuwei was the first of four such garrisons established by the Chinese in the Corridor back during the Han dynasty. From the bus station, we walked north and passed through an opening in the huge city wall the Chinese built 2,000 years ago to keep out the Huns. Just inside the wall, we dropped our gear in the seediest of hotels and rented bicycles. There wasn't any public transport in Wuwei, and the pedicab drivers didn't seem to be willing to pedal foreigners around for less than five times what they charged locals. So we did our own pedaling. We chose for our destination the place where Wuwei's famous Flying Horse was found. The bronze steed was discovered in 1969 along with a host of other items in the tomb of a Han dynasty general. The story behind the Flying Horse of Wuwei is that it represented a real horse that once belonged to the leader of a nomadic tribe to the north, and it was captured by a Chinese general known as Black Tiger. It not only saved the general's life on several occasions, it even saved the life of the crown prince. Horses were the key to military operations in this part of the ancient world, and it is no coincidence that one of them was immortalized in bronze in Wuwei. The Wuwei area is still one of China's major horse raising centers.

The Chinese army's Number-One Shantan Horse Ranch is in the upland pastures of the nearby Chilien Mountains less than fifty kilometers to the west. It's the biggest horse ranch in Asia, occupying more than 10,000 hectares at an average elevation of 2,300 meters, and surrounded on three sides by peaks averaging more than 4,000 meters. It's a bit too cold for your average Chinese, and most of the ranch hands are Tibetans and Mongols. But it isn't too cold for horses, and it has been prime horse country for at least 2,000 years. In fact, that was where the Huns and the other nomadic tribes raised their horses, and that was the first place the Chinese attacked when they decided to take control of the Silk Road. The camel may have carried the merchandise on the Silk Road, but the horse carried the men who controlled, or tried to control, the road. The artistry lavished on Wuwei's bronze horse was minor compared to the care the Chinese spent in raising horses in the hills west of town.

Although the Number-One Horse Ranch was too far for our limited energies, we did manage to pedal to the tomb where Wuwei's famous horse was found. A mere kilometer north of the center of town, we reined in our bicycles and walked down a long corridor that led to the underground chamber where the horse was found. What is there to say about a tomb? It was dark and dank, and maggots had beaten us to the body. The tomb wasn't that noteworthy, except that being the tomb of a Han dynasty general, there was a shrine on top of the grave mound honoring Lei Kung, the Duke of Thunder. This was where officials came to pray for rain or for victory. The Duke of Thunder, it turned out, had a set of magic drums strung around his waist, and if he could be persuaded to beat them, the sound caused clouds to arise and enemies to flee. That was about all people ever talked about on the Silk Road: rain and Huns. Nowadays, it's oil and tourists, and judging from the lack of incense at the shrine, Lei Kung apparently had no control over those.

We remounted our bicycles and pedaled back to town. Along the way, we saw a pagoda. It was about thirty meters high, and there were small bells hanging from the eaves. They sang in the wind and told this story to anyone willing to listen: a long, long time ago, back when relatives of the Huns were getting ready to sack Rome, the Chinese general, Lu Kuang, was sent from Ch'ang-an with an army of 70,000 soldiers to subdue the Silk Road kingdom of Kucha and was ordered to bring back Kucha's most famous citizen, the Buddhist monk Kumarajiva. Kumarajiva's fame as an expositor of Buddhist scriptures had reached the Chinese emperor, and he wanted to hear such expositions for himself. General Lu conquered Kucha, captured Kumarajiva, and headed home. But when he reached Wuwei, the general learned that a new emperor had ascended the throne. Lu weighed his options and decided not to return. Instead, he established his own kingdom, with Wuwei as its capital, and he refused to hand over his prize. So there Kumarajiva sat for the next seventeen years, in the dusty garrison town of Wuwei, until the next Chinese emperor finally sent an army that managed to defeat Lu Kuang and free his famous prisoner.

Nearly twenty years after he set out, the Buddhist monk was finally welcomed in Ch'ang-an. The emperor had Kumarajiva installed in a garden just beyond the palace wall, and he placed 3,000 scholars at the monk's disposal to assist him in his translation work. Kumarajiva, though, hardly needed their help. During his captivity he had become proficient in Chinese and was able to produce translations of Buddhist sutras from Sanskrit that remain among the gems of Chinese literature.

The emperor was so impressed with Kumarajiva's abilities, he decided to conduct a eugenic experiment. He ordered ten ladies of the court to take turns sleeping with the Buddhist monk. Whether or not the monk acquiesced or whether or not the experiment was a success is not recorded, only that whenever Kumarajiva gave a sermon, he told

Stupa containing Kumarajiva's tongue

his audience to take the lotus flower and not the mud from which it grew. And before he died, the monk vowed that if his translations and commentaries in no way deviated from the Buddha's meaning, then his tongue would survive the flames of the crematorium. Sure enough, when he died and his body was cremated, his tongue remained intact.

And that brings us back to Wuwei. Although his ashes were placed in a stupa outside Ch'ang-an, his tongue was sent back to the Silk Road kingdom of Kucha. But once again, Wuwei barred the way, and his tongue never made it home. It ended up inside the pagoda toward which we gazed. Like his tongue, Kumarajiva's pagoda was still there. It was one of the first pagodas ever built in China, and its twelve-tiered form was quite lovely compared to the bigger, plainer structures erected later in Ch'ang-an and elsewhere in the Middle Kingdom. Unfortunately, we were limited to viewing it from the street. The pagoda was no longer part of a religious site. It was now part of the parade ground of the local military police, and foreign friends were not welcome. We paid our respects from the distance and pedaled on.

When it was first laid out over 2,000 years ago, Wuwei was called Liangchou. And the town had played an important role in the history of the region since then. This was all recounted for us, after a fashion, at our next destination, the Wuwei Museum. One of the museum's most important pieces was a stele unearthed in Wuwei two hundred years ago. The stele dated back to the eleventh century, and it had a story to tell.

In the eleventh century, the leaders of a nomadic tribe known as the Topa joined forces with other nomads and established the Hsi-hsia, or Western Hsia, state. The state soon became a dynasty, and it eventually wrested all of Northwest China from Chinese control. That included the Kansu Corridor, and Wuwei became the dynasty's second most important city, second only to its capital in the neighboring province of Ninghsia.

Over the next two centuries, the Western Hsia proved to be a thorn in the side of the Mongols, and Genghis Khan made its destruction his last task. Historians have called the ensuing campaign the most dramatic episode in Mongol history. It ended in 1227 with the death of Genghis and the annihilation of the Western Hsia. Fortunately for Wuwei, its commander surrendered to the Mongols, and the city was spared. The Mongols, though, did their best to obliterate all traces of their former enemy, including their language. And they would have succeeded. But someone buried the stele that began this story and that provided modern linguists with the key to deciphering a language lost for nearly nine hundred years. Just as we were taking all this in, the custodians at the museum told us it was closing time. We were tired anyway. Another long day on the Silk Road ended with a plate of dumplings, a couple cold beers, a hot bath, and bed.

It was just as well. Exploring the city's nightlife would have only led to disappointment. How could it have compared to what it once was? During the T'ang, the biggest public celebration in China was the Lantern Festival, which occurs on the first full moon of the New Year. During one particular lantern festival, Emperor Hsuan-tsung thought he had really outdone his predecessors, and he asked one of his advisors if he had ever seen such a glorious display of lanterns and music and dancing. The advisor was an honest man, and he was also well-traveled. He told the emperor to close his eyes and imagine what sort of lantern festival the gods celebrated in Heaven. The emperor closed his eyes and imagined clouds of incense and light filling the sky and waves of music and dancers swirling through a firmament of stars. When the emperor opened his eyes, his advisor told him he had just seen what the lantern festival looked like in Wuwei.

Wuwei was the funnel through which all the music of Asia entered China, and it was once a city where every other person could play the lute. But we were a thousand years too late. Instead of lutes, all we heard that night was the sound of a cement mixer outside our window. Wuwei was trying to catch up to the twentieth century, and it was late.

走廊

7. The Corridor

THE NEXT MORNING WE BOARDED a bus headed through the narrow strip of land known as the Kansu Corridor. The Corridor is sandwiched between two very different landforms. To the southwest stretch the snowcapped ridges of the Chilien Mountains extending 500 kilometers along the Corridor's entire length. To the northeast are the endless dunes of the Tengger Desert. Tengger is Mongolian for "big sky," of which there is plenty. The Tengger is the fourth largest desert in China, 43,000 square kilometers in area. And Wuwei is a major center of efforts at desert rehabilitation. According to Chinese scientists I

Thin line in the distance is the Great Wall

talked with at the Desert Research Institute in Lanchou during my trip up the Yellow River, China's deserts occupy 10 percent of the country, and the total area is increasing at the rate of 1 percent per year. At that rate, China will be 20 percent desert in another hundred years.

As we headed northwest from Wuwei the next morning, the road led through dunes and our first stretch of gobi. Westerners are often confused when they hear the Chinese apply the term to different areas. Will the real Gobi Desert please stand up? The real Gobi Desert, at least the one cartographers have given the name to, is in Mongolia. The reason these others are masquerading under the same name is that the term "gobi," which the Chinese pronounce "ge-bi," is Mongolian for "stony land." The area north of Wuwei introduced us to a good example of it. At least the road through this particular gobi was good, well-paved and flat, and there was even room for vehicles to pass. Still, it wasn't long before we saw our first roadkill: a man lying facedown at the side of the road, his bicycle a tangled mess. Somewhere in the distance a hit-and-run driver was hurrying home to his family.

As we continued through the desert, on our right appeared one of China's greatest wonders, the Great Wall. The Wall begins at the shores of the Pacific Ocean and extends all the way to the stony heart of Central Asia, or about as far from the ocean as you can possibly get. Most tourists only see the sections that undulate like a gray serpent over the mountains north of Beijing. But the wall in Kansu is just as great. Gone, though, is the serpent. The land here is flat, and the wall is one long line of brown—a five-meter-high line of brown stretching along the east side of the Kansu Corridor for a hundred kilometers between the old garrison towns of Wuwei and our next destination, Changyeh.

This section of the wall was built in the second century BC to keep out the Huns. That was when generals such as Huo Ch'u-ping finally succeeded in chasing the nomads out of the Corridor. Traces of General Huo's old camp were said to be visible south of the town of Shantan. Shantan was the only sign of civilization between Wuwei and Changyeh, and it wasn't much of a sign. This was where the New Zealander Rewi Alley came in the 1920s and set up his first manual arts school. Alley was a leftist missionary and one of the few Westerners who actually weathered the Cultural Revolution in China. He died in 1987, and a museum in Shantan was built in his honor, or so we heard. Our bus only stopped long enough to pick up a few passengers, then rumbled on toward Changyeh.

In the distance, the wall followed us north. The wall not only kept the Huns from China's western borders, it also kept them from the Middle Kingdom's best pastures. The success of the Huns was due in large part to their superior horses, and once they lost control of the mountain pastures in the Kansu Corridor, they lost their advantage over the Chinese. The pastures are still the best in all of China. Not long after leaving Shantan, we passed the turnoff leading to General Huo's old camp and the Shantan Horse Ranch, the biggest horse ranch in Asia and home of horses that can run 500 kilometers in a single day and sweat blood, or so it is said.

But we were bound for Changyeh. Like Wuwei, our next destination owed its existence to the Chinese army. Wuwei was the first permanent garrison established by the Chinese in the Kansu Corridor, and Changyeh was the second. The two towns had other points in common. Wuwei stood guard at the edge of the Tengger Desert, the fourth-largest in China, Changyeh at the edge of the third-largest desert, the Baidan Jaran, 44,000 square kilometers in area, a thousand more than the Tengger. The Baidan Jaran was also the more forbidding of the two, made up of 20 percent shifting sands and 60 percent megadunes. Most sand dunes average less than fifty meters in height, but megadunes average three hundred and extend for several kilometers. Caravans that made it across such a landscape, where the only water was bound to be too alkaline to drink, must have found Changyeh sweet indeed. Its old name was, in fact, Kanchou, "sweet oasis." Wuwei, meanwhile, was known as Liangchou, or "cool oasis." Five hours after leaving the cool oasis, we rolled into its sweet counterpart and checked into the Kanchou Guesthouse, which turned out to be a bitter waterhole, indeed.

Of all the hotels we stayed in during our trip, the Kanchou Guesthouse was the worst, though there were a few close runners-up. For the equivalent of $15, we checked into a room that wasn't as clean as a cattle car on a Chinese freight train. Clouds of dust rose as we walked across the carpet. The beds threatened to collapse. The clerk told us our room included a bathroom, but he neglected to mention that the bathroom didn't include a toilet. And I'm not sure I want to mention the condition of the hole in the floor down the hall. When hot water finally arrived in the bathtub around 9:30 at night, it was the color of consommé. The only thing that worked in the room was the hat rack.

Naturally, we turned our attention to the town. It was still early afternoon when we arrived, and a sign at the entrance advertised bicycles for rent. However, the hotel's two aging two-wheelers were down for the count and didn't look like they would ever fight their way through traffic again. We walked outside and flagged down a pedicab and toured the sights in more comfort than we enjoyed in our room.

Our first stop was Changyeh's most famous sight: the city's Big Buddha Temple. As we entered the courtyard, we paused at a pavilion where several musicians were giving an impromptu concert. Their efforts recalled another concert held in Changyeh more than a thousand years earlier. The year was 609, and musicians came here from every kingdom on the Silk Road along with rulers and ambassadors and everybody who

Changyeh's Reclining Buddha

was anybody. They all came to meet the Chinese emperor. The ruler of China at that time was Emperor Yang of the Sui dynasty.

Three years earlier, in 606, he had toured the newly completed Grand Canal that connected the Yellow River with the Yangtze. It was the grandest procession ever witnessed in China with a string of 500-ton barges stretching for a hundred kilometers. Supplying the royal retinue with provisions devastated the surrounding countryside as well as the court's own tax base. But the emperor had a good time, and he decided to follow up the Grand Canal Tour with a Silk Road Tour.

And so he set off in the year 609. But instead of traveling via Lanchou and Wuwei, he took a more southerly route via the Pingling Caves and Chinghai Province, intending to enter the Kansu Corridor via the Pientukou Pass in the Chilien Mountains. It was early July, and the height of summer, but the Chilien Mountains are like other mountains. The weather can change at any time. And it did. A snowstorm appeared out of nowhere and buried the royal retinue. Thousands of soldiers and attendants froze to death, and the emperor's party must have appeared less than majestic when it finally arrived in Changyeh. But once again, Emperor Yang had a good time. In fact, he enjoyed the music and dancing so much he invited the performers, all 18,000 of them, to the capital and in one stroke changed Chinese music and dance forever.

But that was then. The musicians we heard in the courtyard apparently put the temple's buddha to sleep. Inside the main shrine hall, we found the Silk Road's biggest reclining Buddha. It wasn't an especially aesthetic rendering, but it was, as advertised, plenty big. It was thirty-five meters long from head to toe and was made by constructing a wood frame and wrapping the frame with straw then adding several tons of clay and paint. The Big Fella was made in 1098, and we weren't surprised he was built lying down.

More interesting than the statue was the story of how it came to be built. One day at the end of the eleventh century, a monk heard the strains of music and followed the music to the spot where the temple now stood. But there was nobody there, no musicians, nothing. The music, in fact, seemed to be coming out of the ground. The monk found that most unusual, so he dug into the ground, and lo and behold he discovered a small reclining jade buddha. His discovery seemed so miraculous that the monk decided the spot deserved a temple and the biggest reclining buddha he could muster. And that was how Changyeh's reclining buddha came to be.

In addition to the statue of the Buddha entering Nirvana, the hall included statues of his major disciples. They were gathered behind him, all of them looking distraught at the loss of their teacher. It was such a sad looking group we didn't linger. We returned to our pedicab and proceeded from Big Buddha Temple to Changyeh's second most famous site: the city's wooden pagoda. We could have walked. It was only two blocks away, but we didn't want to give up our transport. Unlike Big Buddha Temple, the pagoda was deserted. No one was even there to sell us entrance tickets. As we walked around the outside, we concluded it was unlike any pagoda we had seen before. First, it was eight-sided, and there were dragon heads at each corner of each story, and there were nine stories, which made seventy-two dragon heads. Second, the structure consisted of a wooden framework filled in with adobe bricks. With its whitewashed walls and exposed wooden beams, it reminded me of German *stockwerk*, and the beams didn't end until they reached the top, thirty-two meters from the ground.

During its heyday, Changyeh's pagoda was so famous among the kingdoms of the Silk Road, it was even mentioned by historians in far-off Persia. Nowadays, it was lucky to be standing at all. We left it the way we found it, in a courtyard overgrown with weeds, and looked for something else to do. We considered the city's drum tower, which we passed on the way into town. It was said to be the biggest drum tower on the Silk Road. But we had seen drum towers before and were looking for something different. Our pedicab driver suggested we visit one of the ethnic minorities on the Silk Road.

It just so happened that sixty kilometers west of Changyeh in the county seat of Sunan is the home of the horseback-riding, mutton-eating, milk-tea-drinking Yuku. China's 1990 census counted 12,000 Yuku, and 90 percent of them were living in Sunan County. Like the

Changyeh's Wooden Pagoda

other minorities along the Silk Road, the history of the Yuku is a history of migration. Their ancestors were a branch of the Huns the Chinese chased out of the Kansu Corridor 2,000 years ago. Around the fourth century AD, this particular branch started calling themselves Uighurs, specifically Yellow Uighurs. They herded horses and cattle and sheep in the grasslands along the northern branch of the Silk Road, near the kingdom of Kucha. But Kucha is a thousand kilometers to the west of where they are now. When Genghis Khan swept through Kucha in the thirteenth century, the Yuku followed his lead and took up Tantric Buddhism. When Tamerlane swept across central Asia two centuries later, the Yuku refused to give up their new faith and fled from the grasslands north of Kucha to the grasslands west of Changyeh.

From his base in Samarkand, Tamerlane had already annexed Iran and Afghanistan and devastated large parts of eastern Turkey, southern Russia, and northern India. His next target was China, and he gathered a huge army at Kucha. The Yuku warned the Chinese authorities about Tamerlane's plans, but the Chinese dismissed the great conqueror as just another border bandit. Fortunately for the Middle Kingdom, Tamerlane suddenly died, and his successor decided against the invasion in favor of the peaceful spread of Islam. If Tamerlane hadn't died, it's quite possible there would be more mosques than temples in China today.

Meanwhile, despite the change in religious policy by Tamerlane's successors, it was too late for the Yuku to return to their homeland, and they settled down to raising horses and yaks and sheep in the grasslands bordering the 4,000-meter-high peaks of the Chilien Mountains. Our pedicab driver introduced us to a friend who drove an actual taxi, and it didn't take long before we were headed for Sunan County. It was already late afternoon, but the driver thought he could get us there and back before dark. Alas, his taxi broke down halfway, and we had no choice but to catch a ride back to Changyeh in a passing truck. No Yuku adventure for us. All we could do was sigh and return to the Kanchou Guesthouse, where we tried to alleviate our misery with cold beer. I don't know how we could have handled the Silk Road before refrigeration.

往前

8. Onward

CHANGYEH WAS ONE TOWN WE WERE glad to leave behind, which we did the next morning on the first bus heading north. As we left, the endless megadunes of the Baidan Jaran Desert were to our right and the snowcapped ridges of the Chilien Mountains to our left. As the road swung slightly west and skirted the edge of the mountains, we passed our first herd of camels grazing in the gobi. No doubt about it. We weren't in Kansas anymore.

These were two-humped camels, Bactrian camels—Bactria being an old name for Afghanistan—as opposed to their one-humped Arabian cousins, and we may as well give them their due while we roll toward our next destination. Nobody knows when camels were first domesticated or which of the two kinds was domesticated first. For nearly 4,000 years, these two beasts of burden have divided the Silk Road between them, with the one-humped Arabian camel proving better suited to the lower, hotter deserts of the Middle East and North Africa, and the two-humped Bactrian camel better adapted to the higher, rockier deserts of Central Asia. The Bactrian camel is shorter and stockier than its Arabian cousin, and its heavier coat helps it survive a greater range of temperatures. Both species have an unusually sensitive sense of smell and can detect plants and water on the wind from miles away. They can also close their nostrils in a sandstorm, and they have double-layered eyelids as well. They may not be the most gainly or handsome of creatures, but, as Arthur Conan Doyle once put it: "You must make allowances for a

Pavilion and stele marking Chiuchuan's Wine Spring

creature which can carry six hundred pounds for twenty miles a day and ask for no water and little food at the end of it."

Four hours after leaving Changyeh, we arrived at the next watering hole, namely the town of Chiuchuan. Although we weren't planning to spend the night, we decided to interrupt our journey long enough to tour the town. After Wuwei and Changyeh, Chiuchuan was the third of the four Silk Road garrisons established by the Chinese. The year was 121 BC and once more the emperor's nephew, General Huo Ch'u-ping, was involved. Huo was responsible for conducting the campaign that drove the Huns out of the Kansu Corridor once and for all, and Chiuchuan was the place from where he launched his final attack. To congratulate Huo on his victory, the emperor sent his nephew a jug of rare wine. Instead of sharing it with his fellow generals, Huo poured its contents into a spring so that his troops could share it. It was a noble gesture, and it wasn't long before everyone started calling this place Chiuchuan: Wine Spring.

Our bus dropped us off at the south edge of town, and we hired a pedicab to take us to see the sights. Naturally, we began with the town's ancient spring. It was still flowing inside a park at the east edge of town just beyond a grape arbor. The spring was full of small, shiny coins, and we wondered what it was about springs and fountains that made people the world over fill them with their loose change. It must be something in our genes. Or maybe it's something in our minds left over from the time when our ancestors honored nature spirits, like the village tree and the village well. In any case, wine was certainly a novel offering, and one that hadn't been forgotten in the ancient town of Wine Spring.

Our next stop was the local museum. It was your typical museum full of stones and bones and busted pots, but it did feature one unusual exhibit that recreated sections of a thirty-three-meter-long mural discovered in 1977 in a fourth-century tomb just outside town. The tomb belonged to a prince, and its murals feature representations of the Chinese world 1,600 years ago: not just the human world, but also the underworld of demons and the heavenly world of spirits, including such favorites as the three-footed crow in the sun and the three-footed toad on the moon.

And what was a crow doing in the sun or a toad on the moon? Well, the sun is the brightest of all things in the universe, and the crow is attracted to shiny objects. And while the sun rules over the sky, the moon rules over the earth, and the toad is attracted to the darkest, dampest recesses of the earth's womb. And why three feet? Because three is the perfect, indivisible number. And that was what we saw at the museum.

Back in our pedicab, we continued into the center of town. One block short of the drum tower, we stopped again, this time at a small factory that produced Chiuchuan's most famous product: "glow-in-the-dark" wine cups. The cups don't really glow in the dark, but they're radiant in the faintest light. They're made of dark green jade that has been carved so thin its veins are transparent. King Mu of the Chou dynasty received a set of these cups when he passed through this region 3,000 years ago. We had to pay for ours, but they were every bit as good. We looked forward to trying them out the next full moon.

Despite its long history as the third of the four garrisons of the Kansu Corridor, Chiuchuan's only aboveground relic from the past was its drum tower at the very center of town. The original tower was built in 346, and from its four gates radiated four roads connecting Chiuchuan with the deserts to the north, the Silk Road kingdoms to the west, the mountains to the south, and Ch'ang-an to the east. The current version was less than a hundred years old and not all that noteworthy. We had our pedicab driver pedal us back to where we began our tour and caught the next bus to Chiayukuan, twenty-two kilometers to the west.

Chiayukuan was the fourth and final Chinese garrison in the Kansu Corridor, guarding the pass that led to Tunhuang. The town's fort was still there, and we planned to see it soon enough. But the town itself was a faceless industrial park full of factories producing fertilizer and iron and cement. The town was so spread out, there was actually a public bus. And it was so prosperous, it had two hospitals, one of which we visited right after we checked into our hotel.

Not long after beginning this trip, I contracted my usual respiratory infection from which I was finally rescued by Finn's four-day supply of tetracycline. Now it was Finn's turn, and the tetracycline was gone. We proceeded to the emergency ward of one of the city's hospitals. It was like a scene from *M*A*S*H*. The smells of urine and disinfectant wafted down the unlit hallway that led us into the waiting room. Finn asked the doctor on duty for antibiotics. The doctor suggested an X-ray. Finn insisted on drugs. The doctor reached over to a tray filled with soapy water and selected a bent needle. Finn ran for the door.

And so we retreated to our hotel, where Finn tried to fight the bronchial infection from which I had just recovered. Since the local hospital turned out to be a farce, if not a nightmare, we threw ourselves on the mercy of a local pharmacy. We were in luck: They had a sulfa-based antibiotic known as SMZ. Finn's fever was soon history, and we were soon using our new glow-in-the-dark cups and toasting the full moon outside our windows with some Chinese brandy.

Chiayukuan began its place in Chinese history as a checkpoint between the newly established Chinese garrisons in the Kansu Corridor

Interior of Chiayukuan Fort

End of the Great Wall at Chiayukuan

and the desert kingdoms of the Silk Road. Over the centuries, its function as a major military garrison increased, and there has always been
some sort of fort there. The next morning, Finn and I hired a car and
went to visit the current version. It was six kilometers west of town on
a bluff overlooking the road that led through the desert to Tunhuang.
To the south were the northernmost snowcapped peaks of the Chilien
Mountains. To the north were the barren red ridges of the Horse Mane
Hills. There was no way a caravan—or an army—could have entered
the Kansu Corridor from the west without being seen from the fort's
ramparts or watchtowers.

This particular version of Chiayukuan's fort was built in 1372, shortly
after the Chinese recaptured the throne from the Mongols and chased
the nomads back beyond the Great Wall. We walked through the fort's
East Gate into the huge courtyard that once held the barracks and offi-
cer's quarters. A small shrine to the God of War was the only structure
still intact. After paying our respects, we climbed the stairs to the top
of the fort's ancient wall and looked out across the desert landscape. A

hundred meters beyond the West Gate was a pavilion where travelers paused for one last look at China.

This was what Chiayukuan was named for. "Kuan" means "pass" in Chinese, and the fort was built to guard the Chiayu Pass. Aside from the Great Wall, it is the most impressive piece of construction along the entire Silk Road. Its outer walls are nearly 11 meters high and 750 meters long, and its inner walls only slightly shorter. At the turn of the last century, two Western travelers who visited Chiayukuan wrote:

> *The scene was desolate beyond words, and if ever human sorrow has left an impress on the atmosphere of a place, it is surely at Chiayukuan, through whose portals for centuries past a never-ending stream of despairing humanity—disgraced officials, condemned criminals, homeless prodigals, terrified outlaws, the steps of all those—have converged to that one sombre portal, and through it have forever left the land of their birth. The arched walls are covered with poems wrung from broken hearts.*

In ancient times, it was the custom to throw a rock at the wall next to the gate through which westbound travelers passed. If the rock bounced back, it meant they would return. If it fell to the ground, they would never see their family again. The section of the wall near the gate was in bad shape, and there was a sign asking people not to throw rocks. And so we dropped ours and proceeded through the archway and along a rough road to where the section of the Great Wall that began at the fort disappeared over the Horse Mane Hills. We walked until we came to a stream beside which an enterprising entrepreneur had set out canvas reclining chairs. And beneath the shade of the corkscrew willows that lined the stream, we sipped sweet tea and yawned. There we were at the end of the Great Wall, and all we could do was yawn.

When the Chinese first extended their wall-building activities into the Kansu Corridor, the Great Wall went past Chiayukuan all the way to Tunhuang. But with the passage of time, the section between

Chiayukuan and Tunhuang was abandoned. And when the Chinese began rebuilding the wall in the fourteenth century, they ended it at Chiayukuan. Ever since then, Chiayukuan, rather than Tunhuang, has been where the wall that began 4,000 kilometers away at the edge of the Pacific Ocean ended.

In honor of the town's connection with this monument to human effort, Chiayukuan had established a Great Wall Museum in the shape of the wall itself. We returned to the car we had hired for the day and asked our driver to take us to the museum. A few minutes later, we were there and viewing reconstructions of the stone sections of the Great Wall in Northeast China near Beijing and the earth sections in the Northwest near Chiayukuan. For those at the western end, the reconstructions showed how each layer of tamped earth was separated from the next by a layer of straw. The straw gave the wall resilience and helped prevent cracks. Other than the reconstructions and a few models, the museum relied on black-and-white photographs with captions in Chinese to tell the story of what is said to be the only man-made object visible from outer space—though no one who has been to outer space has seen it without the aid of a telescope. Despite the effort and the money that had gone into the museum—and it was clearly a well-constructed, well-thought-out museum—we were disappointed. Where were the stories, the battles, the tragedies, the meaning behind such an incredible creation?

Among the stories conspicuously missing was that of the man who built the wall in the first place. Fortunately, I had my own sources for his story. After the First Emperor united central China's warring states in 221 BC, he ordered construction of a wall to protect his empire from the periodic invasions launched by nomadic tribes to the north. He assigned this monumental task to his chief general, Meng T'ien. Meng gathered a force of 300,000 men and marched north 800 kilometers to Inner Mongolia. From there, Meng's forces spread out east and west, and over the next ten years when they weren't battling nomads they labored at linking together sections of preexisting walls with 2,000 kilometers of new walls. The result was one continuous wall stretching 3,500 kilometers from the Pacific Ocean to the upper reaches of the Yellow River south of Lanchou.

Far less known, but almost as impressive, was Meng T'ien's construction of a superhighway connecting the Chinese capital of Hsienyang (just across the Wei River from Ch'ang-an) with the newer sections of the Great Wall in Inner Mongolia. Parts of that road are still visible, though not from space, and range from five meters in width in mountainous areas to twenty-five in the plains. In his spare time, some say Meng T'ien also found time to invent the writing brush without which Chinese calligraphy would be impossible. But for all his achievements, Meng T'ien only aroused the envy of others. When the First Emperor died, the chief eunuch forged a letter ordering Meng T'ien to commit suicide. Meng knew the letter was a forgery and refused to obey. But the First Emperor's successor turned out to be the chief eunuch's puppet and issued a real letter. Meng had no choice. He was buried overlooking his superhighway just inside his Great Wall.

While the town's Great Wall Museum could have done a better job honoring the man responsible for the wall, our disappointment was somewhat mollified by a wing that included the mummified remains of several women. At least, I think they were women. The curator had covered up their chests and groins to keep our natural curiosities at bay. The exhibit also included dozens of painted bricks that once decorated the walls of the tombs where the corpses were found. I noticed that several of the paintings depicted women picking mulberry leaves to feed silkworms, and I wondered if that hadn't been a breach of security. To maintain their silk monopoly, the Chinese went to great lengths to keep the Western World from finding out how the fabric was made. And they succeeded until the sixth century, when the Persians and Indians finally unlocked the secret. Perhaps it was no coincidence that the tombs in which those painted bricks were found were also from the sixth century.

Since our curiosity was aroused and we had nothing better to do, we returned to our car and headed for the tombs that yielded the museum's bricks and corpses. The gobi desert east of town included more than a thousand such tombs. As we approached, they looked like so many waves in a sea of gravel. They dated back more than 1,500 years to a period when warfare and drought decimated Chiayukuan and other garrisons in the area. In recent years, archaeologists had excavated thirteen of the tombs and had opened one of them to the public.

After parking, the caretaker led us to what looked like an aboveground outhouse. But the outhouse turned out to have stairs leading down to a burial chamber far below the surface. The walls were covered with the same sort of painted bricks we had seen in the museum showing the occupant having a good time and being well cared for in the afterlife. But even with the lighting along the ceiling, the underground chamber was dark, damp, and creepy. We couldn't help asking ourselves what we were doing in someone else's tomb. We decided we had better have a cold beer while we still could and returned posthaste to the Chiayukuan Guesthouse.

At $35 a night, the Chiayukuan Guesthouse was one of the most expensive places we had stayed so far. It was definitely overpriced. When we checked in, the clerk defended the high price by pointing to the sign behind the desk. It had two stars on it. China's Ministry of Tourism authorized hotels to charge according to how many stars they received as a result of the ministry's periodic inspections. When the ministry's officials visited the Chiayukuan Guesthouse they must have been blind or bribed. At one point we considered trying to look behind the hotel's sign to see how many stars they actually received, if any. Still, any port in a storm.

Since we were both recovering from bronchial infections, once we were back in our room, we decided on an afternoon of beer and catching up on our journals. One sight we decided to forego was July the First Glacier in the nearby Chilien Mountains. Chiayukuan is in the middle of an incredibly arid landscape, and yet there is a glacier a little more than a hundred kilometers away. It was discovered by Chinese scientists forty-two years earlier on July the First, hence its name. But it was a two-day trip involving more money than we cared to spend and also required a bit of climbing. Instead, after dinner we watched the sun go down and the full moon illuminate the snowcapped ridges of the Chilien Mountains from the comfort of the balcony of our two-star (possibly one-star) hotel. We were glad to be traveling the Silk Road in the twentieth century.

敦煌

9. Tunhuang

T HE NEXT DAY WE FOLLOWED OUR fellow Silk Road travelers, past and present, beyond the Chiayukuan Pass. That was where merchants stopped in ancient times to pay tolls, and travelers stopped to have their papers checked. Once beyond the fort that guarded the pass, they headed into the desert, and many wrote poems of farewell on the fort's walls before heading into the unknown. Nowadays, people still leave poems on the walls, though they aren't quite so ominous or heartrending.

Several decades before us, General Chu Teh came here and left this poem on the walls:

> *Beyond Chiayukuan Pass are fields of oil*
> *on the gobi sands is a new oasis*
> *60,000 people have forged ahead*
> *battling upstream in their quest for glory*

Chu Teh was talking about the new town of Yumen, or Jade Gate, 150 kilometers west of Chiayukuan. Yumen was the site of China's first oil field, where production began in 1938. The 60,000 people Chu Teh mentioned made up the workforce that operated the oil wells in the 1950s. Actually, oil production in that area dated back much earlier all the way back to the Han dynasty, when the Chinese discovered that the black liquid gushing forth from the area's "fire springs" could be lit and poured from garrison walls upon attacking troops.

Our Tunhuang-bound bus bypassed the Yumen turnoff and continued northwest to the town of Anhsi. During the T'ang dynasty, Anhsi was the chief garrison maintained by the Chinese in Central Asia. It was undoubtedly one of the more interesting cities on the Silk Road, but there wasn't anything left from the past. The city was completely destroyed during the Muslim rebellions of the nineteenth century. Our bus stopped only long enough to take on a few more passengers, then left the Kansu Corridor for good and turned west toward the oasis of Tunhuang. We finally left the snowcapped ridges of the Chilien Mountains behind and traded them for the red and gray eroded hills of the Kansu Badlands.

Despite the nine-hour ride from Chiayukuan, Finn and I were feeling good for the first time in days: our fevers were gone. In honor of this change in fortune, Finn remembered our last night in Chiayukuan with this bus-ride poem, which he titled "Breaking the Silk Road Fever":

> *Above the Chilien Mountains*
> *a blooming midnight moon*

brushes a pearly wash
across the shimmering gobi.

I open the broken windows
feel the cool desert breeze
and watch a string of snow white camels
take a long stinging drink.

Nine hours on any bus is a long ride, but it all faded from memory when we discovered cold beer waiting for us at a restaurant next to the Tunhuang bus station. The town was a true oasis, indeed. And right across the street, we found our hotel: the Feitien, or Flying Asparagus Hotel. Actually "fei-t'ien" translates as "flying apsara," an apsara being a heavenly deity that hovers around a buddha and scatters flowers or plays a lute. But I've never been able to say the word "apsara" without stumbling and have taken refuge in "asparagus." My apologies to any apsaras reading this.

So there we were sipping suds across the street from the Flying Asparagus, when suddenly we realized we hadn't eaten all day. We saw potatoes in the kitchen and asked the cook to chop up a few and deep-fry them. He looked puzzled, but he followed our instructions to perfection. And over the next few days we ordered so many plates of chips, he added them to the restaurant's menu. It was, perhaps, our one contribution to East–West exchange on the Silk Road: French fries.

After satisfying our thirst and hunger, we walked across the street and checked into the hotel. The Flying Asparagus was the watering hole of budget travelers, not that it was all that cheap. This was Tunhuang, the destination of every traveler who traveled the Silk Road. But the Flying Asparagus was at least within reason: $30 for a double with a bath. For the budget-minded, the price ranged from $2 to $6 per bed in a room with a shower down the hall. The price, though, wasn't the reason we chose to stay at the Flying Asparagus. Its location across the street from the bus station made it the first place travelers stopped in their search for lodging. And those who ended up staying here were a major source of information

Mokao Caves

on travel conditions not only on the Silk Road but also on the road to Lhasa, which once again had been reopened to foreign travelers.

The bus station across the street also had the only cheap transportation to the Mokao Caves, which was why we and everyone else on the Silk Road stopped in Tunhuang. The caves east of town are, without doubt, one of the world's great repositories of Buddhist art. Their presence makes Tunhuang one of the most worthwhile places to visit in all of China. We bought our bus ticket the night before and just after dawn rumbled out of town on the morning run past fields of marijuana lining the road all the way to the turnoff to the caves.

The marijuana, we heard, was for making rope, not dope. We stayed in our seats, and forty-five minutes after leaving Tunhuang we arrived at the caves. Compared to the rip-off prices charged at China's other major tourist sites, the entrance fee at the Mokao Caves was a reasonable 25RMB. A guide for the day was another hundred, and renting a flashlight cost two more. Thus equipped, we entered the Buddhist vision of paradise led by our English-speaking guide.

In Chinese, "mo-kao" means "none higher." The None Higher Caves aren't that high, but they do contain the height of Buddhist art in China. It all began in the second century BC when the Chinese chased the Huns out of the Kansu Corridor and made Tunhuang the westernmost outpost of their empire. Tunhuang was where the two main branches of the Silk Road met, one from the Central Asian kingdoms to the northwest and the other from the Northern Indian kingdoms to the southwest.

Being the westernmost outpost of the Chinese empire, Tunhuang became the biggest city in the eastern half of the Silk Road, and it grew rich from the trade that passed through its gates. By the second century AD, Tunhuang's population reached 80,000. Not long afterwards, Buddhist monks began arriving in large numbers—partly due to warfare and unsettled conditions in their own lands, and partly due to missionary zeal. It wasn't long before the leading citizens of Tunhuang became fervent believers in this new religion, and to express their faith they financed the construction of hundreds of cave shrines in the area.

The first such shrines at Mokao date from the middle of the fourth century, or about the same time as the Pingling Caves southwest of Lanchou and those on Maichishan southeast of Tienshui. However, the caves at Mokao have done a better job of weathering the depredations of nature, Muslim fanatics, and Western art collectors. Nevertheless, the Chinese are still mad about what happened at Cave 17.

The year was 1905, and the German archaeologist Albert von Le Coq was visiting Hami, the next major oasis to the north. From a merchant, he heard about the discovery of rare manuscripts at Tunhuang, but he was in a hurry to return to Kashgar. He flipped a coin and Kashgar won. Two years later, Aurel Stein followed the same rumor and arrived at Tunhuang to see for himself. Stein had already ransacked a dozen ancient Buddhist sites and carried off cartloads of statues and frescoes to take back to India and England. But at Tunhuang he found his greatest prize of all: the world's oldest printed word in the form of a copy of the *Diamond Sutra* that rolled off the press in the year 868.

The sutra was one of thousands of manuscripts he pried loose from the Taoist monk, Wang Yuan-lu. Wang was the self-appointed guardian of the Mokao Caves, and in the course of making repairs he discovered the manuscripts behind a false wall in Cave 17. Wang was not unaware of the importance of his discovery, and he reported it to the local authorities. But before the authorities could remove the manuscripts for safekeeping, Stein arrived and managed to bribe Wang. For a donation of 130 pounds, Stein bought thousands of the world's oldest books and manuscripts, many of them dating back to the ninth and tenth centuries. The following year, the Frenchman Paul Pelliot paid Wang another 90 pounds for an equally large collection. The Chinese are still furious about the loss of what they have since called one of their greatest national treasures. Most of the library's 15,000 manuscripts are now scattered among the national archives of India, England, and France. Wang needed the money to repair the cave shrines, and Aurel Stein and Paul Pelliot were only too happy to help him out.

Cave 17 is actually a small side chamber of the much larger Cave 16. Both caves were carved out of the sandstone cliff in the ninth century and used as the private shrine halls of a famous Tunhuang monk, which is probably why they were chosen to house the collection of manuscripts two centuries later. The discovery of the manuscripts has had an immense impact on Buddhist literary studies, since it included the oldest known copies of many important Buddhist works. One caveat, though, is in order. Just because a copy is the oldest doesn't mean it's the most useful. In the case of the Tunhuang manuscripts, they didn't really constitute what we would call a library. Most were made to acquire religious merit and include numerous errors made by scribes who made their living copying texts for the pilgrims who came here. Many of these texts were probably never read but simply copied and offered to the temple as so much incense. Still, the Tunhuang manuscripts, as they have since become known, constitute the ancient world's single most important surviving collection of ancient texts, including the world's earliest known form letter for drunks and the hosts who had to endure them.

The letter began:

> *Yesterday, having drunk too much, I was sufficiently intox-*
> *icated to surpass all bounds. However, none of the rude*
> *and coarse language I used was uttered in a conscious state.*
> *The next morning, after hearing others speak on the sub-*
> *ject, I realized what had happened, whereupon I was over-*
> *whelmed with confusion and ready to sink into the ground*
> *with shame.*

The writer went on to suggest an early opportunity to make up for his transgression. And a suitable reply for the host was also included in the manuscript. What an odd piece of writing to stash in a Buddhist sanctuary! But then again, the scribes responsible for the Tunhuang manuscripts were there to serve the needs of pilgrims. And what pilgrim wouldn't want such a letter among their travel gear? I've already made a copy for myself and Finn.

Once our guide completed her account of how China's greatest literary treasure was stolen by foreigners, we moved on to the Mokao Caves' remaining treasures: its wall paintings. The murals of Tunhuang cover the walls of nearly five hundred caves and were painted between the fourth and fourteenth centuries. Even though some of the colors had faded or oxidized, they constitute China's greatest art gallery as well as its richest source of information about cultural exchange on the Silk Road.

Most of the paintings focus on Buddhist subjects, especially on the Buddha's own life, or rather, lives. The engine driving Buddhist doctrine is the law of karma, the law of cause and effect that extends for as many lifetimes as one can imagine. According to Buddhists, everything we do, think, or say is like a seed that sooner or later bears the fruit that makes up our daily round of existence as well as our consciousness. Thus, buddhahood is seen as the result of many lifetimes of effort in performing deeds that produce good karma. And the walls of the Mokao Caves are covered with the good deeds performed by Shakyamuni in his previous lives, deeds such as offering his body to a starving tigress.

The goal of Buddhism, however, isn't better karma. It's liberation from the workings of karma, an end to the endless round of birth and death. This Shakyamuni achieved through his Enlightenment and subsequent Nirvana. And many of the caves at Mokao include a rear niche with a statue of the Buddha's reclining figure as he freed himself from karma once and for all.

In addition to the Buddha's life, another theme that appears in many of the caves is the Buddhist vision of paradise, in particular the Western Paradise of Amita Buddha, where liberation from karma is said to be easier to attain than in this world of pain. To be reborn in his paradise devotees only have to repeat the name of Amita Buddha three times with an unfettered mind: "Amita Buddha, Amita Buddha, Amita Buddha."

Try as we might, Finn and I were still there, not in Hell, but also not in Heaven. As we continued on into the next cave, we noticed that the head of one of the statues was missing, and there was an empty space where there should have been a kneeling statue on the other side of one of the buddhas. And one of the walls was bare. Anticipating our questions, our guide said the missing pieces were taken by Langdon Warner and were in Harvard's Fogg Museum.

Warner came to Tunhuang in 1924 and was just as impressed as Stein and Pelliot had been with the artistic treasures of Mokao. He also sensed their impending doom. In the years since Stein and Pelliot visited, the caves had been ransacked by Muslim fanatics who gouged out the eyes of buddhas. And some of the caves were used as dormitories by White Russians fleeing the Bolsheviks.

Warner was horrified by the damage they had done and proceeded to "save" what he could for the glory of art. Again he greased the palm of the caretaker, our old friend Abbot Wang, who was only concerned that Warner not touch any of his new statues and paintings. He needn't have worried. Warner wasn't interested in Wang's garish replicas.

It wasn't until the 1930s that the Chinese government finally slammed shut the door on the wholesale removal of their country's Silk Road treasures. Given Muslim fanatics, foreigners, and time, there wasn't that much left at other places on the Silk Road, but such were the treasures of

Tunhuang that even now there is more great art here than in any other single place in China. Of the 1,000 caves that historians estimate were once here, nearly 500 had been reclaimed from the encroaching sands of the desert. And of these, over thirty of the best had been opened to the public. We spent all morning and part of the afternoon and could have stayed longer, but there was more to see than art in Tunhuang.

The caves are located along a sandstone cliff at the eastern end of the Mingsha Dunes, which stretch all the way back to Tunhuang and beyond. The dunes, in fact, are forty kilometers long and twenty kilometers wide, and if we wanted to experience what it would be like to cross the desert by more traditional means, this was as good a place as any. Most visitors, however, limit themselves to forays three kilometers south of Tunhuang where one of the dunes looms 250 meters above the surrounding sand. After returning to Tunhuang, that was where Finn and I went next.

For a modest fee, people could ride to the top of the Mingsha Dunes on the back of a camel. We opted to hike, which turned out to be much more difficult than it looked. Our feet kept sinking in the sand. We finally gave up and slid back down then walked over to the "lake."

"Mingsha" means "singing sand." I thought the name might have come from the sound the wind made when it blew across the dunes. But according to local legend, the sound comes from the echoing cries of people buried here by a sandstorm long ago. Singing sand isn't the only attraction. There is also a small lake in the shape of the crescent moon near the foot of the dune. And that's its name: Crescent Lake. Naturally, there's a story that goes with it.

A long, long time ago, a drought struck the Tunhuang area. Wells dried up, trees died, crops withered, and the people wept with grief. One day the beautiful and merciful Cloud Maiden just happened to be floating by in the sky and heard the pitiful cries of the people. She was so moved, she began to cry, and where her tears fell to the ground a pool formed, and the people rejoiced. But not for long. The appearance of a pool of water in the middle of his dunes angered the Sand Demon, and he summoned a storm and filled up the pool with sand. The people once more felt the anguish of their impending doom. But Cloud Maiden wasn't about to give up so easily. She flew up to the sky and asked the Moon Goddess if she could borrow her magic disk. It was only the fifth day of the month, and the Moon Goddess told Cloud Maiden to wait another ten days until the moon was full. But Cloud Maiden said by then the people of Tunhuang would be dead from thirst.

The Moon Goddess was moved by Cloud Maiden's desire to help the people, and she agreed. Cloud Maiden returned to the dunes with the moon in her sleeve, and when she laid it on the sand, it turned into a crescent-shaped lake. Seeing this new threat to his realm, the Sand Demon summoned his forces once more. But this time to no avail. Every time the sand rolled down the dunes to fill up the lake, a mysterious wind arose and blew the sand back up onto the dunes. And the wind was still blowing, and the crescent-shaped lake was still there, and so was the sun-bleached shrine to Cloud Maiden, who saved the good people of Tunhuang from the Sand Demon a long, long time ago. Seeing all this only made Finn and me thirsty. We returned to the Flying Asparagus for cold beer and a hot bath and were asleep before dark.

The next morning, we hired a taxi driver and ventured forth again to see a few more sights, the first of which was a small white stupa at the edge of town. In addition to guarding China's western flank, Tunhuang was strategically located at the junction of the northern and southern branches of the Silk Road. Among the travelers who arrived here via the northern branch was the Buddhist translator Kumarajiva. We had already seen the stupa that contained his tongue in Wuwei. This stupa was also connected with him.

According to the good citizens of Tunhuang, when Kumarajiva came to their city, he arrived on a white horse, and soon afterward the horse fell ill. The horse had been Kumarajiva's faithful companion through many hardships, and the monk tried everything to revive the ailing steed. Kumarajiva even slept beside his horse. All to no avail. Then one night when the horse seemed about to breathe its last, it opened its mouth and said, "Master, I am really a white dragon from the Western Sea. But because the road from your homeland was so hazardous, I

Stupa containing remains of Kumarajiva's horse

Tunhuang movie set

vowed to carry you to China so that you could spread the Dharma. From here the road is smoother, and there are inns along the way. I shall go no farther. Let us say farewell."

There was a blinding flash, and when Kumarajiva regained his senses, all that remained was the horse's white skin. In memory of his companion, Kumarajiva erected a stupa over the remains. It's still here, its whitewashed bricks still shimmering in the desert sun, and its bells still tinkling in the desert wind, and visitors still come to pay their respects to the white dragon of the Western Sea.

After adding our bows to those who had come here before us, we headed west out of town. In addition to the Mokao Caves east of town, Tunhuang had a new attraction in the other direction, twenty kilometers to the west. It was a model of an ancient Chinese Silk Road city. It was built by a Japanese film studio for use as a movie set. The Japanese never do anything halfway and spent the equivalent of half a million dollars making sure their set looked the part. The name of the movie was, appropriately, *Tunhuang*, and it was filmed here in the summer of 1987.

The movie was set a thousand years ago in the Sung dynasty, and it follows the career of a young man who failed the imperial exams that would have assured him of an easy life as an official. Instead, he ended up in Tunhuang enduring the hardships of life on China's western border.

As we approached, our driver pointed out a thin, black line on the horizon. In a matter of minutes, the line became a blanket that darkened the midday sky and filled the air with stinging sand. The wind blew people off their bicycles and cars off the road, and it lasted more than two hours. Even in the safety of our car we were covered with fine dust. Finally, the wind slowed. Even though the dust was still thick enough to make visibility difficult, our driver continued on.

When we finally arrived at the movie set the place was deserted. There weren't even any Japanese tour groups. We pushed open the huge gate, paid the admission fee, and strutted down the main street like a couple of gunslingers caught in a time warp. A couple of horses cowered against a mud wall trying to keep out of the wind. The saloon was empty, so was the teahouse. We climbed the steps that led along the wall and shielded our eyes against the swirling sand. Somewhere to the west was the edge of the empire.

When the Chinese first established a garrison at Tunhuang 2,100 years ago, they extended the Great Wall another hundred kilometers beyond it, just to make sure they wouldn't have to get out of bed in the middle of the night. We climbed back down and headed for the edge.

Since we had the whole day and weren't in a hurry, we decided to make a stop on the way. Fifteen kilometers after leaving the movie set, we turned off the highway and drove two kilometers across trackless gobi to the edge of a rift valley. From the parking lot at the edge of the valley, we walked down a set of steps to a series of caves that overlooked the Tangho River. The Mokao Caves east of Tunhuang are also referred to as the Eastern Thousand Buddha Caves, and these are known as the Western Thousand Buddha Caves.

The gate was locked, but our yells finally brought the caretaker around. He let us in and took us to the office. The man in charge said

Ladder to Western Thousand Buddha Caves

the place wasn't open to tourists, but he proceeded to sell us tickets anyway, then led us to the caves. There were about twenty of them. They were smaller and the paintings that covered their walls simpler than their counterparts east of Tunhuang. But the art was every bit as good. In fact, Chang Ta-ch'ien, one of China's most famous twentieth-century artists, spent several years in these very caves perfecting his drawing and coloring techniques. We spent an hour then hit the road again.

We continued heading west until suddenly a small oasis came into view. A stream of crystal-clear water flowed along the roadside then into vineyards and orchards. Just beyond the oasis there was a rise in the desert landscape, and on top stood the surviving beacon tower of Yangkuan Pass. The road ended just below the tower. Two thousand years ago, when the Chinese established Tunhuang as the westernmost city in their empire, Yangkuan Pass became their final outpost, the edge of the Chinese empire beyond which only Buddhist pilgrims and merchants dared venture.

The pass is seventy-five kilometers west of Tunhuang and is one of two established west of Tunhuang where the two branches of the Silk Road parted. For centuries the Chinese got their finest jade (or yu) from the kingdom of Khotan at the foot of the Kunlun Mountains. Hence, the pass through which the jade arrived became known as Yu-men, or Jade Gate. Later, in the Han dynasty a second pass was established to prevent caravans from avoiding the road toll or invaders from outflanking Jade Gate. Because the second pass was to the south, it was called Yangkuan ("kuan" meaning "pass" and "yang" meaning "sunny" and hence "southern").

Of the two, Yang Pass stirs deeper emotions. Try to find a Chinese person who hasn't heard this eighth-century poem Wang Wei wrote upon seeing off a Silk Road–bound friend at a village near the capital:

> *Morning rain dampens the dust in Wei Village*
> *new willow catkins have turned the inn green*
> *drink one more cup of wine my friend*
> *west of Yang Pass there's no one you know*

View from Yangkuan Pass

Finn and I scanned the horizon. Wang Wei was right. Beyond the pass was no one we knew.

Although Yang Pass marks the westernmost outpost of the Chinese empire, this doesn't mean the Chinese didn't make attempts to extend their dominion beyond it. One such attempt was the establishment of a garrison at Loulan four hundred kilometers to the west in the middle of the forbidding wastes of the Lop Desert. The Buddhist travelers Fa-hsien and Hsuan-tsang made it across that desert, as did Marco Polo, though all three were convinced the place was haunted. The Venetian noted that travelers crossed this desert in large groups for protection. And such were the mysterious changes in the landscape itself that before travelers went to sleep at night, they posted signs pointing in the direction they were headed, lest they start off in the wrong direction the next morning.

Despite the Lop Desert's reputation for swallowing those who tried to cross it, the Swedish explorer Sven Hedin made his greatest discovery there. In 1901, while following the Tarim River to where it empties into the great salt lake of Lop Nor, Hedin stumbled onto the ruins of Loulan. After sifting through what was left of the place, Hedin was able to piece together a fascinating picture of life in a Chinese garrison 2,000 years ago. In 1914, Aurel Stein also visited the Loulan ruins and conducted his own excavations. In addition to materials written in Chinese, Stein discovered thousands of documents in the ancient Indian Karoshti script suggesting that Loulan was not only an outpost of China. At some point in its history, it was also an Indian outpost.

The Lop Desert is also home to other mysteries. Beginning in the 1960s, the Chinese used it to test their nuclear weapons. Naturally, it was off-limits to the likes of us. But we did consider a side trip to Yumen, or Jade Gate. Although it was known as the conduit through which much of the finest jade entered China, this was the pass through which silk left China on its journey to the rest of the world. It was also the pass through which the secret of silkmaking left China. In ancient times, the people of Khotan who mined the jade so loved by the Chinese had an equal passion for fine silk. But as time went on, Khotan produced less and less jade, and the king worried that soon there would not be enough jade left to buy silk.

The king finally came up with a solution. He requested the hand of a Chinese princess in marriage and secretly sent word to her to bring silkworm eggs and mulberry seeds to supply the needs of her new home. The guards at Jade Gate searched her luggage and even her clothes, as well as her servants, and their clothes. They found nothing, and the princess was allowed to continue on. When she reached Khotan, the king asked if she had done as he had requested. She said she had. The king was surprised, and he asked her how she had managed to smuggle the eggs and seeds past the guards at Yumen. "Easy," she said, as she undid her hair. And that was how the secret of silkmaking left China and reached the rest of the world.

But while the road that led through Jade Gate was the main conduit for jade and silk, it was the most difficult and dangerous part of the Silk Road. Most travelers avoided it. The road often disappeared beneath the constantly shifting sands of the Lop Desert, and it was still not open to foreigners. Most travelers followed the route leading north from Tun-huang through the Mohoyen Desert to the oasis of Hami.

The northern route was also the route chosen by the Chinese monk Hsuan-tsang. But instead of waiting to join a caravan before continuing on, Hsuan-tsang entered the Mohoyen Desert with a single guide and a single horse. Not only was the desert itself a threat to his safety, one night his guide approached the sleeping monk with a knife, intending to kill him and steal his money. Hsuan-tsang must have been under the Buddha's protection. Suddenly he awoke and sat up in silent medita-tion. Deeply moved by the monk's obliviousness to personal danger, the guide fell to his knees and asked the monk's forgiveness. He also advised Hsuan-tsang to turn back, that there was no water ahead. But the monk refused. Instead, he gave the guide money and enough food and water to return to Tunhuang, while he continued on alone.

Not long afterwards, Hsuan-tsang ran out of water, and for five days he drank not a single drop. He was dying of thirst and almost uncon-scious when his trusty steed finally led him to a pond of fresh water. Hsuan-tsang rejoiced, and eventually he arrived safely at the oasis of Hami, which was our next destination, too.

哈密

10. Hami

AFTER ONE MORE NIGHT AT THE Flying Asparagus, Finn and I walked across the street and took the morning bus to the train station in Liuyuan. The size of the oases on the Silk Road always surprised us. It took our bus more than thirty minutes to get past Tunhuang's fields and pastures. Finally, we were back in the desert again—this time a desert of rolling black hills and sagebrush flats. Despite the dryness of the landscape, a light rain began to fall, and the temperature began to drop. By the time we reached Liuyuan three hours later, we were freezing—and it was early September.

We took the bus to Liuyuan because it was on the train line between Lanchou and Urumchi, the capital of Hsinchiang province. Four or five trains passed through every day, and we managed to squeeze onto the noon express. There were no seats, but there were berths in the soft sleeper section, and we indulged ourselves. After a few minutes, the conductress came by to check our IDs. She was from Harbin in Northeast China, and for the past few years she had been in charge of one of the express trains that ran between Lanchou and Urumchi. She said it took two days and two nights, and the turnaround time was nine hours. Then it was another two days and two nights back to Lanchou. After every roundtrip, she was given seven days to recuperate before her next run. She had been working for the national train system, she said, for more than twenty years, and her monthly pay was the equivalent of $40. That might have impressed someone in China twenty years earlier, but nowadays it was close to poverty wages. The amount we paid for two soft sleeper berths to the next oasis was as much as she made in a month.

After traveling through the Kansu Corridor and visiting the Han dynasty garrison towns of Wuwei, Changyeh, Chiuchuan, Chiayukuan, and Tunhuang, we finally left Kansu sometime during the night and entered the province of Hsinchiang—a name that means "new territories." Early the next morning, we waved good-bye to the conductress from Harbin, as our train left us standing on the station platform in Hami. A few blocks away, we checked into the Hami Guesthouse. In a very real sense, we had left China, or that part of China dominated by the Han Chinese. In Hsinchiang, the Han Chinese are the minority. And they probably wouldn't be here at all if it hadn't been for another tribe of barbarians.

In the seventeenth century, the nomadic Manchus swept down from their homeland near Korea and succeeded in conquering China and gaining control of the dragon throne. This marked the beginning of the Ch'ing dynasty. When China's neighbors began calling Manchu authority into question, the Manchus put the question to rest at the beginning of the eighteenth century by defeating the Mongol khan, whose control had extended into eastern Turkestan and Tibet. In one fell swoop, the Manchus, and thus the Chinese, gained control of the regions now encompassed by Hsinchiang, Chinghai, and Tibet for the first time in Chinese history. And in the Chinese orbit they have remained—not without, of course, occasional protests and even uprisings by the native populations.

Most of the world has heard about the ethnic unrest in Tibet since the Chinese "liberated" that country forty years ago. But such unrest has been far greater, though less publicized, in Hsinchiang, where the Muslim minorities have been far more willing to risk bloodshed in an effort to reassert their autonomy.

Up until we rolled into Hami on the express, we had seen people in every Silk Road town wearing skullcaps of various colors. Usually they were white and occasionally black or dark green. Such caps are part of Muslim traditional dress, and there are Muslims in every town in China. But in Hami, the number of people wearing these caps approached that of the uncapped. We were in China in name only.

The population of Hsinchiang in 1992 was over fourteen million. Of that number, six million, or 45 percent, were Uighurs, and five million, or 40 percent, were Han Chinese. The Uighurs have been here for a thousand years. The Han Chinese are recent arrivals. A few came with the Manchus as merchants or administrators three hundred years ago, but most were ordered here to colonize the country's new frontier during the Cultural Revolution in the 1960s and '70s or were lured there in the '80s with promises of easy money. The Uighurs weren't altogether happy about their new neighbors. But they didn't have much choice. During our journey through the province, we didn't see a single Uighur policeman, and the only officials we met were Han Chinese. The authorities call Hsinchiang the Uighur Autonomous Province, but it is autonomous in name only.

In ancient times, the Chinese had another name for Hsinchiang. They called it the Western Region. West of China was a land of mystery and a land whose people came and went with the wind. The Chinese first noticed the Uighurs more than 2,000 years ago. The Chinese called them Tinglings. At that time, the Tinglings were herding sheep north

Uighur herding goats down Hami's main street

of Mongolia on the shores of Lake Baikal. In the ensuing centuries the Tinglings were forced to move, first to avoid the Huns then to escape the Turks. During these centuries of constant migration, the Tinglings allied themselves with other tribes to keep from being swallowed up or annihilated. In the Turkic language, the word for "ally" is "Uighur," and the Uighurs of today are the descendants of these allied tribes.

In the eighth century, the Uighurs finally got their century of glory on the stage of Central Asia, and the Chinese finally stopped calling them Tinglings. In a series of lightning battles, the Uighurs swept the Turks from China's northern borders once and for all. And if it hadn't been for Uighur assistance in putting down rebellions, China's T'ang dynasty would have ended in the eighth century instead of in the tenth.

But Uighur power didn't last long. By the tenth century they had been replaced on the Central Asian stage by other nomads, including the Mongols. But what saved the Uighurs from the dustbin of history was that during their moment of glory, many of them exchanged their nomadic way of life for life in town. They also exchanged religions.

During that brief period when they controlled most of Central Asia from their base in Mongolia, the Uighurs wore their hair long, and they bowed to the sun, instead of Mecca. Then one day in the eighth century, while the Uighur khan was doing a bit of pillaging near the Chinese capital, he met a group of Sogdians who had come to China from Persia. The khan was so impressed with their spiritual powers that as soon as he returned to his base, he ordered his followers to accept the religion practiced by the Sogdians. The Sogdians were devotees of the third-century Persian prophet Mani. They were Manichaeans.

Mani taught that all of creation was a combination of light and dark and that the path to divinity lay in shedding our dark material natures for the light of the spirit. This, people could do only through a lifetime of purification. Practitioners intent on experiencing permanent union with the divine light we see at death were enjoined to eat no meat and drink no liquor, not even beer, and to sleep alone. Others, of weaker dispositions, were enjoined to practice charity.

The Uighurs thus became the only ethnic group in East Asia to practice Manichaeism. But they didn't stay Manichaeans very long. Between khans, they toyed with other faiths, including Nestorian Christianity. Obviously, the Uighurs were just browsing. But they finally put their money down two centuries later when Islam arrived on the Silk Road. And today it is hard to find a Uighur—aside from the Yellow Uighurs of the Chilien Mountains—who isn't a Muslim. The reason for this change in faiths was that when other nomads swept the Uighurs from the Mongolian Plateau, the only Uighurs who remained were those who had given up their nomadic way of life for the settled life of the Silk Road oases. And the Uighurs just happened to be there when Tamerlane arrived in the fourteenth century and gave them a choice between Islam and death. The Uighurs were no fools. And after Tamerlane left, they decided they liked their new faith. So there we were in Hami, in our first Uighur town and also our first Muslim town.

We had seen Muslim men wearing caps before, but in Hami we saw our first Muslim women—although we didn't see that much of them. Their faces were hidden beneath their purdahs, or shawls. And they wore long dresses and heavy brown stockings like our grandmothers

Mausoleum of Muslim missionary

used to wear. The town of Hami, itself, looked an awful lot like its women. There wasn't that much to see. But there was something. Not long after we arrived, we rented bicycles from an obliging lady just outside the entrance of our hotel. After asking directions, we worked our way through the old part of town and pedaled south. We didn't have to pedal far. After one kilometer, the road passed a cemetery. We stopped, parked our bicycles, and walked up a trail to a mausoleum at the top of a small hill.

The mausoleum belonged to Kai-ssu, one of three Muslim missionaries who came to China in the first half of the seventh century, shortly after the death of Muhammad in 632. One Muslim missionary traveled by sea and died in Canton, and the other two came by land and died on the Silk Road. Kai-ssu died at Hsing-hsing-hsia, a day's journey east of Hami. In 1945, his remains were moved to Hami, and local Muslims erected the mausoleum with its adobe walls and green-tiled roof. The place was surrounded by enough weeds to suggest that not many people visited.

We returned to our bicycles and pedaled one more kilometer to another cemetery—this one enclosed by a gate. This is the most sacred place in the region and the scene of huge celebrations on Muslim holy days. As many as 10,000 worshippers take part, and as many as 5,000 manage to squeeze into the cemetery's mosque. Ancient poplars and thousands of tombs cover much of the surrounding countryside, but the only tombs of significance are two mausoleums just outside the mosque. One is a monolithic structure and was missing most of its tiles. The other was recently rebuilt out of adobe and wood. Both mausoleums belonged to the Uighur kings who ruled Hami between 1700 and 1930. When the last Uighur ruler died in 1930, Han Chinese bureaucrats moved in to fill the vacuum and precipitated a rebellion that spread across the entire province. If Hami impresses visitors as a faceless town, it's because the government leveled the old Ch'ing dynasty town in retaliation and replaced it with the same mindless architecture we had seen everywhere else in China.

On our way back from the tombs, we passed through what was left of the old town, whose poorly paved streets were lined with crumbling adobe walls. Through open gates, we saw people in clothes our grandparents might have worn, sitting on mats drinking sweet tea in the dappled shade of grapevines. The pace was different, more suited to the Silk Road. But the old way of life was clearly disappearing. Everywhere the walls were covered with posters advertising the latest fashions and products of a new order.

Except for the tombs of the Uighur kings and a glimpse at how Uighurs used to live, there wasn't that much to see in Hami. Out of boredom, we pedaled to the local museum, which we finally located in the second floor of a nondescript yellow building. It wasn't open, but persistence prevailed, and we managed to track down the lady with the key. Hami was once one of the most famous towns on the Silk Road, and we were wondering how it had ended up in such a sad state.

When China first extended its influence into Central Asia in the second century BC, Hami was just beyond its reach. In those days Hami

Tombs of the last Uighur kings

was known as Yiwu. During subsequent dynasties, China's authority in the area waxed and waned. Sometimes Hami, or Yiwu, fell under its control, and sometimes the control of other ethnic groups. It was the most important oasis between Tunhuang and Turfan. And not only did the northern branch of the Silk Road pass through Hami and continue south to Tunhuang and the Kansu Corridor, another branch veered east at Hami and continued across Mongolia to Beijing. It was the shortcut to North China. Considering its strategic importance, Hami must have been quite wealthy, and we were surprised at the dismal state to which it had sunk. But that was before we visited the local museum, where a display case provided the answer. It was a topographic display that lit up, and when we pressed the button for the Han dynasty, Hami was suddenly seventy kilometers to the west. That was all we needed, and that was where we headed the next morning on a bus full of coal miners bound for the town of Santaoling.

The highway on that part of the Silk Road was still under construction, and the bus had to zigzag its way through a series of detours.

It took nearly two hours to go two-thirds of the way to Santaoling. Finally, it let us off at a windswept place where a paved road led south to Wupao and the ruins of Hami's incarnation as Yiwu. Before continuing on, the driver warned us that the morning bus to Wupao had already passed through, and the afternoon bus wouldn't get us back to the highway in time to catch the last bus back to Hami. No problem, we thought. China was a great place to hitchhike. We waved good-bye and waited for vehicles heading south. For the next two hours we threw rocks to kill the time. We were in the middle of nowhere and going nowhere fast trying to hitchhike on a side road that led to the site Hami occupied 2,000 years ago. We were only fifty kilometers west of the current Hami, but we may as well have been in the middle of the Gobi Desert. We stood there in the freezing wind waiting for anything with wheels, but the only vehicles that passed by in the direction of Wupao were two tractors, a jeep, and a motorcycle.

After two hours, we finally gave up and decided to return to Hami. Five minutes later, we were riding in the backseat of a new Peugeot. It still had all the plastic on the seats and doors, and it had that new-car smell. The driver was a young Han Chinese who worked for the coal mine at Santaoling. He had been everywhere in the Hami area, and he told us about the ruins we hadn't been able to visit ourselves.

The ruins, he said, were barely visible in the fields just outside the village of Ssupao. In the Uighur language Ssupao was called Lapchuk, and according to local historians Lapchuk was the ancient site of Hami, or Yiwu as it was once known. Over the past thousand years, Hami had moved steadily eastward following changes in the water supply, and, according to the man who rescued us from our plight, there wasn't anything worth seeing at Lapchuk. On our way back to Hami, he suggested the next time we found ourselves in this part of the Silk Road, we should visit Palikun instead. Palikun is on the other side of the Tienshan Mountains that rose like a gigantic white wall thirty kilometers to the north. Unfortunately, we had a date with an evening train. Still, there's no reason why we shouldn't let our imaginations pay Palikun a visit while we wait.

Finn and author waiting in vain for ride to Yiwu

In Chinese, "Tien-shan" means "Mountains of Heaven," and their peaks extend west from Hami all the way to Uzbekistan. For the past several hundred years, the north side of the Mountains of Heaven have been home to the Kazak minority, and before that it was home to the Mongols, and before that the Uighurs, and before that the Turks, and before that the Huns. I suppose if a person wanted to see how nomads lived in China, the Palikun Grasslands would be about as good a place as any.

There was a road to Palikun that crossed the Tienshan Mountains just north of Hami, and there was even a daily bus. To the rest of the world, Palikun is known as Barkol, which is the name of the lake just west of Palikun. According to the *History of the Latter Han Dynasty*, that was where the Huns retreated each time the Chinese chased them out of the Kansu Corridor, and from where—once they had regained their strength of numbers—they would attack again. It wasn't until the second century that the Chinese put a stop to their raids once and for all by depriving the Huns of Palikun. And following their victory, the Chinese extended their beacon towers to Palikun to make sure they wouldn't be surprised again. The Chinese had a system of signals (smoke during the day, fire at night) that enabled them to transmit messages hundreds of miles in a matter of minutes. "Hello, Tunhuang, this is Palikun. No sign of Huns. But we are a bit thirsty out here and could use another caravan of beer." Imagine trying to say that with smoke or fire.

While we were waiting for our train we also stocked up on Hami's most famous product. To the Chinese, the name Hami is synonymous with melons. Hami melons have been the most famous melons in China ever since one of Hami's Uighur kings sent some to the Chinese emperor in thanks for leaving him alone. That was less than three hundred years ago. Hami had been producing melons, though, for at least 2,000 years.

When most people think of Hami melons, they think of the light-green variety about the size of a cantaloupe. But Hami produces dozens of varieties. Among the current favorites are Crispy Red Heart, Old Ironskin, Cannonball Yellow, and Black Eyebrows. I'm not sure why Hami's melons are so good. It must have something to do with the summer sun. Hami is located in a depression only 750 meters above sea level, and summer temperatures often exceed forty degrees Celsius, or one hundred degrees Fahrenheit. Whatever the reason, Hami melons possess an exceptional fragrance and sweetness. But melon season, which lasts from July to September, was over, and Finn and I had to make do with preserved melon slices—which were surprisingly just as fragrant and just as sweet as the fresh variety. The chefs of Hami have also developed a number of recipes featuring their town's most famous product. In addition to such gourmet dishes as Heavenly Mountain Snow Lotuses and Silver Waves in the Red Sea, there is Hami melon rice, Hami melon noodles, Hami melon steamed buns, even Hami melon wontons. Can Hami melon pizza be far behind?

吐鲁番

11. Turfan

T HE EVENING EXPRESS TO TURFAN finally arrived at eight o'clock, only an hour late, and rescued us from China's melon capital. At the station, we were only able to buy standing room tickets. But once on board, we proceeded to the conductor's cubicle. On most trains, the cubicle is located next to the dining car. But because the express was so long, this time the cubicle was three cars away. By the time we found it, there was already a crowd and a lot of pushing going on, but we finally saw an opening, fought our way through, and lo and behold the conductor sold us two berths in the soft sleeper section.

We slept all the way to Tahoyen, where we disembarked at 4:30 in the morning. The train line didn't go to Turfan but passed by sixty kilometers to the north on its way to the provincial capital of Urumchi. From Tahoyen, travelers had to take the bus into Turfan. We walked outside and found it parked right in front of the station. The driver was asleep under a huge sheepskin coat. Another prospective passenger said the bus wouldn't be leaving until six-thirty. We thought that odd, as there were no more trains due. But he was right. Two hours later, at six-thirty, the driver finally stirred, and a few minutes later we were off. It was still the middle of the night. Six-thirty in Hsinchiang wasn't even close to dawn. It was closer to four-thirty. To keep everyone marching to the same drummer, the Chinese government decreed that in China all time was Beijing time. From Turfan, Beijing was 2,500 kilometers to the east, but it was the same time in both places. While people in Beijing were doing their t'ai-chi and out walking their birds, we were rolling across a black landscape under a starry sky.

It was after eight when we finally pulled into Turfan, just as the sun was coming up. Actually, we didn't quite pull into Turfan. The bus stopped a few kilometers short of Turfan, and everyone had to pay for their tickets before we could proceed. That shouldn't have taken long, but the problem was that the conductress insisted foreigners pay double, and several of the other foreigners on the bus objected. Fortunately, Finn and I had our teacher IDs and avoided the whole mess. Still, we had to sit there for an hour while East met West. Finally, money changed hands, and a few minutes later we arrived at the Turfan bus station.

Unlike Hami, where developers had reproduced their vision of life in architectural purgatory, Turfan had maintained much of its traditional character—which was evident as soon as we walked outside the station. On the sidewalk, several white-bearded Muslims were sitting cross-legged on prayer mats reading passages from the Koran and waiting for new arrivals to leave enough spare change in their alms bowls so that they could make it through another day.

On the other side of the street a huge bazaar was just opening up. Donkeys were delivering cartloads of apricots and grapes, and more white-bearded men were unlocking the shutters of their stalls, revealing an assortment of knives and teapots and silken shawls. The streets were lined with irrigation canals and covered by the cool shade of date trees and grapevines. We felt like we were finally on the Silk Road.

After walking a few blocks and taking in the early morning goings-on, Finn and I flagged down a taxi and asked the driver to take us to a hotel. There were only two places foreigners were allowed to stay in Turfan. Tour groups and travelers of means stayed at the Oasis Hotel, and everyone else stayed at the Turfan Guesthouse. We chose the Guesthouse, though we had our doubts about our choice when we arrived. It was being renovated, and to get to the bathroom we had to leave the building where our room was located, walk across a courtyard, turn down an alley, and try to remember which dark doors led to the holes in the ground. And did we remember to bring our flashlight, and which of the dark doors led to the water faucets masquerading as showers?

The staff, though, was friendly. Looking back on our stay there, we agreed we made the right choice. The Guesthouse was right across the street from John's Cafe, and as soon as we awoke from a morning nap, we enjoyed the rare pleasure of a cup of coffee and an omelette. It wasn't the greatest coffee or the greatest omelette, but in the middle of the Silk Road it was the thought that counted.

Actually, we had been looking forward to this. We first heard about John's Cafe from other travelers at the Flying Asparagus in Tunhuang. John was a young Han Chinese who lived in Kashgar, at the western edge of the Chinese empire, and he was a good example of how attuned citizens of the Silk Road were to business opportunities. He discovered that it paid to cater to the tastes of travelers such as ourselves.

Several years earlier, John borrowed some money from friends and relatives and opened his first cafe in the courtyard of the Seamen's Hotel in Kashgar. Then the year before our visit, he opened his second cafe in Turfan, and he planned to open a third cafe in Tunhuang later that year to complete his goal of spanning the Silk Road with his own oases. His choices were apt: Tunhuang, Turfan, and Kashgar were the three most worthwhile places to visit on the Chinese section of the Silk Road, and they were already attracting the bulk of foreign tourists.

In addition to coffee and omelettes, John offered other Western favorites like fried potatoes, as well as a few basic Chinese dishes. The menu also included apple pie and chocolate mousse. But the food wasn't the main reason foreigners flocked to John's. His cafes were located outdoors under grapevines. It was just the sort of atmosphere Silk Road travelers looked for and unfortunately found so seldom.

But the pleasant atmosphere in Turfan wasn't restricted to John's Cafe. Adobe was still the preferred construction material, and Turfan was worth walking around. After breakfast, we took a stroll. It turned out to be a bit longer than a stroll. But it was still a stroll. From John's we followed a dirt lane through one of the oldest sections of town and past hundreds of typical Uighur homes with their adobe outer walls and inner courtyards covered by trellises of grapevines. Gates were usually left open during the day, and one of the families invited us inside for a cup of tea, Uighur-style—sweetened by rock sugar, dried fruit, and nuts. The family was so hospitable, they invited us to stay for lunch, but we told them we had sights to see. We were headed for the minaret. And that was where our walk ended: at the Emin Minaret, which is not only Turfan's most famous sight but easily the most beautiful piece of architecture in all of Hsinchiang.

The word "minaret" comes from the Arabic word "manarah," meaning "lighthouse," which is what a minaret looks like. But a minaret serves to summon rather than to warn. From a balcony near the top, the muezzin calls the neighborhood faithful to prayer. Hence, the minaret is an essential part of every mosque, and a mosque is an essential part of every Muslim neighborhood.

We had seen minarets before, but nothing quite like this one. Considering the millions of Muslims in the country, the Emin Minaret should have had more competition. But it was the only truly impressive example of Islamic architecture we saw in all of Hsinchiang. It was built in 1777 by the local ruler Emin Hoja, hence its name, and was designed by a local architect who had seen similar structures in Afghanistan during a pilgrimage to Mecca. In contrast to the square base and different levels of a Buddhist pagoda, the Emin Minaret tapers skyward from a circular

Emin Minaret

base, its surface covered by adobe bricks arranged in more than a dozen patterns. But why, we wondered, was it here?

When we asked the caretaker, he said the minaret was a monument to Uighur support for the Ch'ing dynasty in its dispute with other nomads to the north. Translated into current lingo, the minaret stood as a shining symbol of the centuries-old friendship between the Uighurs and the Han Chinese, which was why it had endured while other examples of Islamic architecture that didn't symbolize such friendship hadn't fared as well.

The minaret was built out of sun-dried bricks at a cost of 350 kilos of silver. Obviously, Emin Hoja was well compensated for his friendship. It looked like a missile aimed at Heaven and tapered skyward for thirty-seven meters to a set of small windows where the muezzin still calls the faithful to prayer—though only on Fridays and holy days. The rest of the week, the minaret and its adjacent mosque are open to tourists like ourselves (although not the staircase leading to the top. That is kept locked.).

After paying the minaret and its mosque a visit, we sampled the grapes that hung from a trellis near the entrance and bought some raisins from a vendor. Then we walked back to the Turfan Guesthouse along the same dirt road that led us there. Back at John's we had an early lunch then experienced the rare pleasure of a long afternoon nap to go with our early morning nap. Afterwards, John's once again provided the perfect setting for dinner. And as the sky turned dark, we had chocolate mousse for dessert and a couple shots of Johnnie Walker to wash away the dust of the road and the sweetness of the mousse. We were finally living the life we had envisioned for ourselves on the Silk Road.

The next morning, we decided to venture farther afield. Outside our hotel, there were a number of private minivan drivers waiting to take people on a tour of the area's attractions. The price for a full-day tour was 150RMB, or less than $30 for five people. We found a van with three people already inside and took the last two seats. It was a deal we couldn't pass up.

The tour began with the sights east of town, which were, according to the guide who sat in front with the driver, best visited in the morning

Flaming Mountains and Journey to the West shrine

when the air was still cool and the sunlight less intense. The first sight was the area's most famous: the eroded red slopes of the Flaming Mountains that begin just north of Turfan and extend east for a hundred kilometers along the highway leading back toward Hami. There wasn't a tree or a blade of grass in sight. On a hot summer day, the surface temperature was said to exceed eighty degrees Celsius, hot enough to fry an egg, or a monk—which brings us to another story about Hsuan-tsang, the monk who passed through the Flaming Mountains on his way to India.

Following his return to China in 645, Hsuan-tsang wrote an account of the lands through which he had passed. Nine hundred years later, his account was transmogrified into China's most beloved fable: *Hsiyouchi*, or *Journey to the West*, in which Hsuan-tsang was joined by four disciples—the most prominent of whom was Sun Wu-k'ung, the Monkey King.

According to this retelling of Hsuan-tsang's journey, when the band of pilgrims reached this part of the Silk Road, they were prevented from going any farther by a wall of flames that extended as far as they could see. What to do? While the monk prayed to the Goddess of Mercy, the Monkey King came up with a more practical solution. He flew off to

Bezeklik

borrow the magic fan of Princess Iron Fan. Although the princess was not very obliging, the two fought a battle of wits, and Sun Wu-k'ung won. He returned with the fan, put out the flames, and the pilgrims proceeded on their way.

We had an easier time. Forty kilometers east of Turfan, we turned off and followed a ribbon of asphalt through the flames. The scenery turned fantastic in its combination of erosion and desolation. Adding to the unreality of it all was a river of clear water flowing out of the gorge into which we now drove. The water came from the Tienshan Mountains fifty kilometers to the north, and we couldn't help wonder how it managed to arrive here without evaporating or disappearing into the desert sands.

We followed the stream's grass-lined shores ten kilometers, until suddenly in the middle of nowhere we arrived at our first roadside attraction. It was an adobe–and-paint recreation of *Journey to the West* depicting the passage through these mountains centuries earlier of the monk and his jolly band. Like any roadside attraction, it tried to make up in novelty for what it lacked in artistic merit.

Actually, it wasn't in the middle of nowhere. Another kilometer down the road—where the road ended—was a place whose name was on the lips of every foreign devil who dared the hardships of the Silk Road a hundred years ago. The name was Bezeklik. And it had a few stories to tell. "Bezeklik" is Uighur for what we would call an "art gallery." It was, in fact, a repository of Buddhist art, and until 1905 it had pretty much been forgotten. The man who rediscovered its treasures was the German archaeologist von Le Coq. When von Le Coq first found his way here, he was not especially impressed with what he saw. Many of the caves had been used for shelter by local herders, and most of the paintings that once decorated their walls had been damaged beyond repair by the smoke from their fires. But von Le Coq kept poking around, and at the northern end of the cave complex, he made his most momentous discovery. The caves at that end of the gorge had been buried by the sand that was constantly slipping down the mountain on its way into the river below. Von Le Coq started digging away the sand, and as the sand fell away he found caves containing hundreds of paintings in perfect condition with colors as fresh as if they had just been painted. In addition to the standard array of Buddhist figures, there were Indian and Persian princes and even a red-haired, blue-eyed barbarian.

Von Le Coq resolved to remove every painting. And this was how he did it: first, he placed a felt-lined board against each painting then cut around it with a sharp knife until he penetrated the layers of clay, camel dung, straw, and stucco on which it was painted. Then he inserted a specially made saw and sawed the innermost layer free from the cave wall. Finally, the board, which now supported the painting, was gradually lowered until it was horizontal with the ground. Then he packed up the painting and sent it to Berlin. His collection was one of the finest treasures ever looted from the Silk Road. Unfortunately, it suffered badly from Allied bombing during the Second World War, and what survived has since been housed in that city's Museum of Indian Art.

There wasn't much left of the caves themselves. The entire northern section where von Le Coq did his "work" was off-limits, and the southern section held only a few hints of what was once here. While we worked our way down the long flight of stairs into the gorge that housed the remains, I couldn't help but think back to von Le Coq's account of his stay here—in particular, one moonlit night "when all was still as death and ghastly howls suddenly resounded as though a hundred devils had been let loose." Von Le Coq and his assistant leapt out of bed, grabbed their rifles, rushed outside and discovered to their horror the whole horseshoe-shaped gorge filled with dozens of wolves baying at the moon. His men assured him that the wolves were harmless, but he shot one anyway. He noted in his diary that sometime earlier he had met a pretty twelve-year-old girl who was betrothed against her will to a man of sixty. As the wedding day approached, she ran away across the desert toward the next oasis. As she did, she stopped at a spring and fell asleep and was discovered by wolves. All that her parents found were bloodstained pieces of her clothing and her boots with her feet still inside.

Sadly, the depredations of foreign devil art collectors and Muslim fanatics left us with little to see at Bezeklik, except, of course, for

Kaochang ruins

the fantastic setting. The caves were carved into the west wall of a sandstone gorge that opened up just enough for a small settlement of Uighur herders. To the north, beyond that most desolate of landscapes, rose the snowcapped peaks of the Tienshan Mountains, the source of the water running through that forbidding world. It was no coincidence of nature that caused the water to find its way here, nor was it chance that led the monks here to carve out the caves and fill them with art 1,500 years ago. The water was led here from the distant mountains by an underground canal, channeled through the gorge, and then into the surrounding desert to the south. The reason the local inhabitants went to so much trouble was that 1,500 years ago there was more than desert in the desert. A few kilometers south of where the gorge met the desert was the ancient city of Kaochang, the capital of the kingdom of Turfan and the place from which the monks came who carved out the caves.

After viewing what was left of their efforts at Bezeklik, we followed the river back out of the gorge and into the desert to the ruins of the

Kaochang ruins

ancient city whose rule once extended five hundred kilometers to the east and the west. Kaochang began life in the first century BC as a small garrison established by the Chinese to prevent the Huns from gaining control of this section of the Silk Road. But it was too far from Ch'ang-an for the Chinese to control very long. Over the centuries, Kaochang grew to become the capital of an independent state, with rulers of mixed Chinese and central Asian ancestry. Like Tunhuang and Hami, Kaochang was situated at converging branches of the Silk Road—one branch of which came from over the Pamirs via Kashgar and the other from over the Russian steppe. Kaochang grew wealthy from trade, and its interests often conflicted with those of China.

On one such occasion, Kaochang's independent policy caused the Chinese emperor to send an army to attack the city. When the ruler saw the Chinese forces approaching, he had a heart attack and died of fright. Ironically, it was the same ruler who welcomed Hsuan-tsang earlier during the monk's journey to India. Hsuan-tsang's fame had preceded him, and once the ruler had heard the monk preach, he said he couldn't possibly let such an eminent cleric leave his city. Kaochang was one of the most sophisticated cities on the Silk Road, and it was at the height of its glory when Hsuan-tsang visited in the seventh century. However, Hsuan-tsang wasn't about to stop halfway to his goal, and he declined the ruler's offer. But the ruler was equally determined, and he only relented when Hsuan-tsang went on a hunger strike.

After disembarking from our van near an opening in Kaochang's ancient wall, Finn and I went looking for the place where Hsuan-tsang stayed. Along with the Buddhist art of Tunhuang, the ruins of Kaochang are one of the highlights of a trip on the Silk Road. Nowhere else in China are such ruins so accessible, so extensive, or so impressive. And nowhere else can modern visitors get a feel for the look and the layout of a Silk Road city. Although as a habitable city it was destroyed by the Mongols in the thirteenth century, the adobe walls of hundreds of its structures have weathered the winds of time.

During his excavations here in 1905, von Le Coq discovered an underground chamber that contained the corpses of more than a hundred monks who were killed by the city's Mongol conquerors. But von Le Coq discovered more than Buddhist art and corpses. He also unearthed the remains of a Nestorian church with a Byzantine-style mural depicting a Palm Sunday procession. And in a Manichaean church, he found a life-size portrait of Mani, the religion's founder. He also found Manichaean manuscripts that revealed to the world for the first time the history and doctrines of that unique and now vanished sect.

Kaochang was a cosmopolitan city where the latest news from Baghdad and Rome was exchanged for the latest gossip from the Chinese court in Ch'ang-an. To walk among its ruins was an unforgettable experience. The ruins were located inside the city's old wall that extended more than five kilometers. Due to the size of the city, many visitors chose to visit the sights by donkey cart. Finn and I decided to get some excersise. And thanks to the cart tracks, it wasn't hard to find the sights.

One sight that caught our attention was a Buddhist shrine hall at the southwest corner of the city. Much of the interior was still intact, including the walls and the huge central pillar around which pilgrims once walked while chanting. When Buddhism first developed as an organized religion, the only religious structure they used was the stupa—which was a mound of earth and later bricks erected over the remains of the Buddha or one of his more eminent followers. Since it was the custom to honor such remains by walking around them, a brick-lined walkway and a roof were added to enable pilgrims to pay their respects regardless of the weather. Eventually, the stupa was transformed into a huge central pillar with a statue of the Buddha in a niche at its base. And finally, not long after Buddhism reached China, the pillar was replaced by an altar and dominated by increasingly large statues of the Buddha. The shrines inside the caves at Tunhuang give a hint of such a development, but at Kaochang the function of the central pillar and walkway are much clearer. As Finn and I walked around the pillar of the shrine hall, we couldn't help but feel we were walking in the footsteps of Hsuan-tsang.

After about an hour, one pile of adobe bricks began to look pretty much like the next pile. Also, the sand was so deep it wasn't easy to walk. Finally, our guide called us back to our minivan. It was time to move on. A few minutes later, we stopped again. There weren't any ruins, but there were tombs. These were the Astana Tombs, just north of Kaochang. "Astana" is Uighur for "capital city," and the tombs are where members of the capital's elite were buried between the fifth and tenth centuries. The region where the tombs are located is China's equivalent of Death Valley, with only slightly more rainfall than the moon. The extreme aridity of the area had helped keep the bodies buried here in a remarkable state of preservation. In some cases, the pupils of the corpses were still distinct when they were first found. But archaeologists found more than bodies, they also found all kinds of clothing and even prepared foods such as dumplings and pastries that provided a fairly complete inventory of what the material side of life was like on the Silk Road 1,500 years ago.

More than five hundred tombs were uncovered here, and three of them were opened to the public. Of course, there wasn't anything to see aboveground. We had to walk down a narrow staircase that led twenty feet below ground level, and it was dark. The caretakers didn't seem to be interested in turning on the lights, except for tour groups—and only for those wise enough to pay the proper amount of baksheesh. This was, after all, the Silk Road. Over the entrance to tomb number three, a plaque recorded the generous donation by a local travel company of 5,000RMB, the equivalent of nearly $1,000—which must have guaranteed the company a lifetime of well-lit visits. Fortunately, Finn and I remembered our flashlights.

Most of the artifacts discovered in the tombs had been removed to the provincial museum in Urumchi, but there were a couple of well-preserved corpses and a number of wall paintings. One of the paintings, in particular, is worth mentioning. It was a picture of a man and a woman each with one arm wrapped around the other and their other arms holding a compass and a carpenter's square. The lower halves of their bodies were also entwined, but not as human bodies, rather as the serpentine bodies of two snakes—or dragons. Naturally, there is a story about who they were.

A long, long time ago, in fact, back when time began, Chaos split into yin and yang, and these split again, and before long the first creature appeared. Its name was P'an-ku, and it was also the world's first workaholic. As soon as it stepped out of the womb of the universe, it picked up a mallet and chisel, and it chipped away for 18,000 years until it created the space between Heaven and Earth in which we all live today. Then P'an-ku dropped dead.

But before it died, P'an-ku gave birth to a set of twins that were half-human and half-dragon. P'an-ku called the boy Fu Hsi—we had already visited his hometown of Tienshui—and the girl was called Nu-wa. Even though they were siblings, they became husband and wife and gave birth to the race of dragon people we call the Chinese—which is why their pictures are sometimes on the walls of graves in which Chinese were buried, even out here on the Silk Road.

We viewed what we could with our flashlights, but before long it was time to return to the surface and head back to Turfan. After a break for lunch at John's, the one-day tour continued. This time, we drove thirteen kilometers west of town to another set of ruins: the Chiaoho ruins, where we arrived just as the daily wind that descended on Turfan every afternoon was beginning to blow.

The name "Chiaoho" means "where rivers meet." Actually, there is only one river, the Yarnaz. But it divides just north of the ruins, and two kilometers later its two branches reconverge just south of the ruins. The ruins themselves occupy the summit of a leaf-shaped island of wind-blown loess 1,700 meters long and no more than three hundred meters across at its widest point. Both sides of the island are lined by sheer cliffs about thirty meters high, and the only way for ordinary mortals to get to the top is to walk up a steep trail that begins just above where the river's two branches meet. Not long after Finn and I started up, we had to stop to tie bandanas across our faces so that we could breathe something other than the sand that swirled across the island and against our faces.

With its natural protection from enemies as well as its easy access to water, the island provided a perfect refuge for the early inhabitants of the Turfan area, and Neolithic remains have been found here dating back over 3,000 years. When the Chinese first arrived about 2,000 years ago, Chiaoho was already the capital of a small kingdom, and its fortunes paralleled those of Kaochang, under whose shadow it waxed and waned. Like Kaochang, Chiaoho was also destroyed by the Mongols in the thirteenth century. Since then it has been home to little more than the wind.

Due to its natural limitations, Chiaoho was never as big as Kaochang, and its population never numbered more than 5,000 or 6,000, about one-tenth Kaochang's, but it was one of the more prosperous cities on that part of the Silk Road, and its ruins were in far better shape than those of its bigger neighbor to the east. After hiking up the trail that led to the top, we passed through what used to be the city gate, leaned into the wind, and continued down the main street. In ancient times, the street was the city's main marketplace and was lined with shops and stalls. It was ten meters wide and extended 350 meters into the heart of the city, ending at the front steps of the city's biggest Buddhist temple.

Chiaoho ruins

As we walked down the street and around the ruins on either side, we were surprised by the number of temples and stupas covering the summit. Chiaoho was only 1,700 meters long and less than three hundred meters across, but we counted a dozen temples and twice as many stupas. Apparently, during one of its later phases Chiaoho's main function must have been that of a religious sanctuary. The ground was littered with shards of T'ang dynasty temple tiles, among the oldest and cheapest souvenirs on the Silk Road, we reckoned.

Following our visit to the windswept ruins of Chiaoho, we asked our driver if we had time to go to the dunes for the cure. Yes, the cure. What with all of this traveling, we were developing a few aches that needed the attention of China's one and only Desert Sanatorium. During the summer, when everyone else in China is looking for an escape from the heat, the blistering sand of Turfan attracts people in need of the area's unique heat treatment. In ancient times, Turfan was called Huochou, or Fire City, which was not inappropriate. Turfan is located in the lowest depression in Asia, just a notch above Hell. And every summer, Turfan's Sha-liao-suo, or Desert Sanatorium, opens up in the dunes sixteen kilo-

Temple ruins at Chiaoho

meters northwest of the city. There, for a modest fee, people suffering from rheumatism and a host of other ailments are examined, diagnosed, buried in the sands, and baked like a bunch of pigs at a Hawaiian luau. But it isn't just the heat that contributes to Turfan's incredible cure rate of up to 90 percent (in the case of rheumatism); the gray sand that makes up the dunes is highly magnetic and helps restore the lines of force running through a person's body.

And if you're worried about skin cancer, never fear: the whole time you're cooking or lining up your ions, you're wrapped tight and shielded from the sun by multicolored tents or beach umbrellas. The pictures we saw made the whole thing look like a surfers' convention gone terribly haywire. Waiting for a wave that never comes. It certainly didn't come for us. The sanatorium, our driver said, was only open between mid-June and early August, and we arrived in mid-September. Alas.

Another alternative, if we had more time, might have been a visit to Aitinghu Lake, forty kilometers to the south. The lake is in the heart of the Turfan Depression more than 150 meters, or 500 feet, below sea level, making it the second-lowest place on any continent, second only to the Dead Sea in Israel, at nearly 400 meters below sea level. Depending on the amount of water that reaches it via the Yarnaz River, the lake sometimes covers as much as 150 square kilometers. Millions of years ago, Aitinghu was one of the largest freshwater lakes on the planet, a thousand times bigger than it is now. But that was before the uplifting of the Indian Plate closed the lake's access to the sea and also ended Central Asia's access to the moisture of the Indian Ocean's monsoons. Ever since then, Aitinghu has grown smaller and smaller as its water continues to evaporate and its concentration of mineral salts continues to increase. During the winter, when Aitinghu freezes, workers drive out onto the lake surface, dig up the ice, and truck it to a nearby factory that turns it into Glauber's salt for use in detergents and medicines. Frozen or not, the lake is said to be strangely beautiful. The Uighurs call it Moonlight Lake. But our driver said we didn't have enough time for a visit, unless we wanted to arrange for a private excursion the following day. The following day, though, we were planning on leaving Turfan, so back we headed to town.

Halfway there, we stopped one last time. In summer, Turfan is one of the hottest places on the planet, and on any given day it's the hottest place in China. In an average year, the temperature of the ambient air exceeds forty degrees Celsius, or 104 degrees Fahrenheit, for more than forty days. In such a place, water is the key to human survival. But where does it come from, we wondered? It comes from, we found out, the distant Tienshan Mountains, but it never sees the light of day. It comes from a system of underground canals that extend all the way from the mountains and include openings for drawing water every ten or twenty meters. This is the karez system, as it was called by the Persians who invented it 3,000 years ago, and whose merchants spread the knowledge of it eastward along the Silk Road.

There have been underground canals in the Turfan area for at least 2,000 years, and by the end of the twentieth century Turfan boasted 5,000 kilometers of underground waterways. Just beyond where our driver parked, we walked down a staircase to see one of these canals. It was an amazing sight. During the summer, the surface temperature could be an egg-frying eighty degrees Celsius, and a few steps below ground, village women were drawing water from a babbling stream right here in Fire City. And the air was cool. We lingered as long as we could, until our guide said it was time to bring the one-day tour to a close.

In addition to being known as the hottest place in China, Turfan also has a reputation as one of the wettest places. I'm not talking about rainfall, but wine. Turfan, it turns out, was responsible for introducing the Chinese to grape wine. The good people of Turfan acquired their knowledge of grapes and grape wine from the same people as the karez system, and they passed it on to the Chinese as part of their annual tribute as early as the seventh century.

Every autumn they packed their sweetest grapes in lead-lined chests together with snow from the Tienshan Mountains. Despite the 2,500-kilometer journey, the grapes arrived in the Chinese capital as fresh as when they were picked. They were received by the emperor and his court with great delight, but an even greater reception was reserved for the wine. It was viewed as such a rare commodity that the emperor only gave it to his favorites. One such favorite was the T'ang poet Li Pai, whom the Chinese still call the Sage of Wine. After one imperial banquet, the Sage distilled these immortal lines from Turfan's newly arrived amphoras, which apparently didn't arrive alone:

> *Wine squeezed from grapes*
> *goblets made of gold*
> *brought here on horseback*
> *with a maiden of fifteen*
> *her eyebrows painted black*
> *her shoes of crimson silk*
> *her accent somewhat strange*
> *her singing sweet as honey*
> *dining on turtle-meat*
> *drinking all she wants*
> *what would she be like*
> *behind the scented curtains.*

Pass the wine, Li Pai.

And so our one-day tour ended, and we returned to our hotel. We had seen just about everything we had hoped to in that pearl of an oasis: the ancient ruins, the ransacked caves, a landscape straight from Hell, the minaret, the underground canals. There was, though, one final pleasure, and it was right outside our window at the Turfan Guesthouse. It was the Uighur song and dance show held almost every night under the grape trellises of the hotel's central courtyard. Visitors can pay money and sit in a chair, or they can watch for free through the vines. All Finn and I had to do was open our window.

Listening to the music, we couldn't help but hear the other end of the Silk Road. We could just as easily have been in Iran—well, maybe not under the present regime. It was remarkable, though, how easily music moved along with more tangible merchandise on the Silk Road. It would be impossible to write about Chinese music without including extensive references to the music of the peoples who lived in what the Chinese once called the Western Regions.

The Chinese came up with the zither, or ch'in, but they got most of their musical instruments from the Middle East, including such typical Chinese instruments as the harpsichord, or yang-ch'in, the two-stringed violin known as the nan-hu, and the lute, better known as the p'i-p'a. Many of their most distinctive musical styles also arrived via the Silk Road. Even the music and ritual dance movements used for more than 2,000 years to honor Confucius on his birthday have been traced to Bactria, home of the two-humped camel. And so, as our time in Turfan ended, we listened to the same music Li Pai no doubt listened to in Ch'ang-an, and we drank the same grape wine he also enjoyed during those brief years when he was a favorite of the court. Alas, Finn and I had tickets on the morning bus to Urumchi. It was with reluctance that we closed our window and drifted off to sleep.

烏魯木齊

12. Urumchi

O UR TICKETS WERE FOR THE eight-thirty bus to Urumchi. However, the bus schedule was more of a wish list. Our bus sat in
the station parking lot for an hour after it was scheduled to leave. At
least we had seats. The bus was packed. Turfan was one of the most
Uighur towns in the province, and the bus was full of white-capped,
white-bearded old men and green-scarfed, brown-stockinged women
with what looked like all their worldly possessions. It took forever to
squeeze everything and everyone on board.

Finally, the bus driver came out of the station, and he was joined by two other drivers who were returning to Urumchi. Finally, we said good-bye to Turfan. Once underway, we rolled across a gobi desert for an hour and a half then entered a gorge that led through the southern branch of the Tienshan Mountains. It was a dangerous road with the usual assortment of close calls and narrowly avoided head-on collisions. The drivers, all three of them, were Han Chinese, and they took turns amazing each other with their derring-do. The other passengers began to voice their concern and yelled at the drivers to stop taking chances with our lives. But their yells had no effect. Finally, after an hour of close calls, we came out of the gorge and stopped for lunch at a restaurant in the middle of nowhere. But the Uighurs on board were so angry at the antics of our drivers, they refused to get out. While they fumed, Finn and I walked down the road to photograph the main range of the Tienshan Mountains visible across the plain to the north.

Just then a Land Rover pulled up across the road from us, and three foreigners got out and started climbing on the rocks. We walked over and exchanged introductions. They were American geologists who had come there to study the extent and dates of glaciation in that part of Asia. One of them, it turned out, shared a college office with a friend of Finn's who once wrote a novel about driving a car off a cliff just to hear it crash. Finn and I wondered if that was a sign. If it was, we had no business getting back on that bus.

But get back on board we did. We didn't feel like waiting for the next bus, assuming there was another one that day. At least the road was fairly straight, and the drivers calmed down. And so we finally rolled into Urumchi on the Turfan mystery bus: you never knew when it was going to leave or if or when it would arrive. This time it arrived, and we found ourselves in the provincial capital with more than a million other people—which was about a million more than there were at the beginning of the twentieth century. After exiting the bus station, we caught a taxi and headed for the venerable Hungshan Hotel next to Hungshan Park. "Hungshan" means "red hill," and that was about all it had to say for itself. Our room was modest, but at least it was reasonable at

$12, and that included hot water. In any case we only planned to stay one night. While we were checking in, we met a young chap selling tickets for the daily bus to Heaven Lake, and within minutes of arriving we arranged for our exit. To make sure we wouldn't have to spend any more time in Urumchi than necessary upon our return, we walked down the street to the airline office and also booked two tickets to Yining. Yining was on the Russian border, at least what used to be the Russian border. Nowadays, the other side was called Kazakhstan.

Thus armed with tickets out of Urumchi in two different directions, we proceeded to the Friendship Store another block down the street and stocked up on all the wine we could carry. Among our discoveries were the Pearl of the Silk Road and Loulan Red, both two bucks a bottle. Loulan Red turned out to be a luscious cabernet, and the Pearl was no less worthy. The people of Hsinchiang had been making grape wine for 2,000 years, but it had taken them that long to figure out they didn't have to add sugar.

The next morning we left Urumchi on an early bus just after sunrise and headed north then east. Being the capital, Urumchi is also the biggest industrial armpit in the province, and it took us half an hour to get out of town and onto the open road. Once we did, we saw herds of camels munching on what was left of summer and gangs of ravens dining on the previous night's roadkill.

An hour and a half after leaving Urumchi, just past the town of Fukang, we turned onto a side road and headed south, into the mountains. Ever since we arrived at the oasis of Hami, the Tienshan Mountains had been silhouetted against the horizon just outside our bus or train windows. They were now in front of us and getting closer, and it didn't take long before we began winding our way into their valleys and up their slopes.

Within minutes the landscape changed from dry grasslands to evergreens and patches of snow. Two and a half hours after leaving the industrial purgatory of Urumchi, we pulled into the parking lot of Heaven Lake. On exiting the bus, the same man who sold us our tickets led us first to a small restaurant where we dined on mutton, then over a small

Our Lake of Heaven yurt

Lake of Heaven and Tienshan Mountains

grass-covered hill to one of his family's lodgings. We were in Kazak country, and our home for the next two nights was going to be a yurt.

"Yurt" is a Turkish word for "dwelling." And that's what it was, although it was quite a bit different from what we were used to. Our guide lifted the flap of a domed tent of felt that was stretched over a lattice framework made from willow branches. Inside, we dropped our bags and bottles of wine on a floor covered with carpets. We were less than three hours northeast of the provincial capital, but it was a world away, and not far from Heaven.

Tienchih, or Heaven Lake, was just outside our yurt. It was aptly named, a blue jewel 2,000 meters above sea level surrounded on three sides by the 5,000-meter peaks of the Tienshan Mountains. From the doorway of our yurt, we watched the sunset turn the snowcapped peaks gold and the lake's water pink.

We weren't the first visitors to enjoy the view from here. Three thousand years ago, King Mu left the Chinese capital and traveled along the Silk Road to meet a woman ruler known as Hsiwangmu, the Queen Mother of the West. And some historians think their meeting took place on the lakeshore just below our yurt.

The identity of the Queen Mother of the West is still a mystery. Some scholars think she might have been the Queen of Sheba in what is now Saudi Arabia. Others say she was the ruler of a kingdom that encompassed parts of what is now Afghanistan and Uzbekistan. The important thing is that for the early Chinese the Queen Mother of the West was viewed as the earthly representative of the Moon Goddess, whose counterpart was the Sun God, or the Lord of the East.

Just as the sun rises in the east every day, the moon reappears every month as a crescent on the opposite horizon. As the Moon Goddess, the Queen Mother of the West also represents the cult of immortality, and the elixir she dispenses to her favorites was presumably what led King Mu to undertake his incredible journey. If you'd walk a mile for a camel, how far would you walk for an elixir guaranteed to extend your life indefinitely? Altogether, King Mu traveled over 10,000 miles, but the elixir didn't work. He was buried just outside Sian.

Meanwhile, from the doorway of our yurt we watched the sunset fade and the stars gather in the sky like snowflakes. It was time to climb under our pile of blankets. Earlier, not long after we arrived, our hosts came and added a few lumps of coal to the iron stove in the middle of our yurt. But we were too lazy to keep the fire going. Besides, we brought our own heat from the Friendship Store in Urumchi, and while we poured ourselves two more glasses of wine, someone in the next yurt began singing a Kazak song.

This shouldn't have come as a surprise. Our hosts were herders who brought their sheep to graze at Heaven Lake every summer. And ever since the Chinese built a road to the lake, the Kazaks had been putting up extra yurts for visitors like ourselves. But it was mid-September, and in another two weeks they would be taking down their yurts and returning to the grasslands at the foot of the mountains to spend the winter in adobe huts.

Next to the Uighurs and Han Chinese, the Kazaks are Hsinchiang's third largest ethnic group with more than a million members. Nearly all of them are scattered along the grasslands bordering the northern branch of the Tienshan Mountains, from Lake Barkol north of Hami all the way to the Ili Valley and the border of the former Soviet Union.

The Kazaks are nomads, and like all nomads they live with and off their flocks. As far as historians can tell, Kazaks have been riding horses and herding sheep for at least 2,000 years, and since we brought plenty of wine, we may as well hear the story about how one of their ancestors married a Chinese princess back when the Senate still ruled Rome. In fact, Cleopatra was still a baby when the Chinese sent their famous Silk Road traveler, Chang Ch'ien, to this part of Asia to establish an alliance with the ancestors of the Kazaks known as the Wusun.

The Chinese were anxious to create a second, western front in their ongoing war against the Huns, who were still threatening their interests in the Kansu Corridor. The Wusun were the most populous of the many nomadic tribes of Central Asia at that time, with an estimated 600,000 members, and Chang Ch'ien was aware that they were unhappy about losing some of their best pastures to the Huns. To cement relations, the

Chinese emperor sent his own sixteen-year-old sister to wed the aged Wusun king, who reciprocated with a thousand of his best horses. And so Princess Hsi-chun, or Willow Waist, became the first link between the ancestors of the Kazaks and the Chinese.

Princess Willow Waist didn't exactly appreciate her new home. Sitting in her yurt, she composed her famous "Song of the Yellow Swan":

> *My family married me to the far end of Heaven*
> *to the distant realm of the Wusun king*
> *my home is a tent my walls are of felt*
> *my diet is meat and mare's milk my drink*
> *memories of the past burden my heart*
> *please yellow swan carry them home*

Not long after their marriage, the king died, and Princess Willow Waist was married to the new king, and soon after that, she died.

Thus began the friendship between the Kazaks and the Chinese, and I think we'd better have another glass of wine. Over the succeeding centuries, the Wusun confederation intermingled with other nomad groups, including the Turks, the Uighurs, and the Mongols, and finally, in the fifteenth century, they formed their own independent tribe to escape the Mongol rulers of the Uzbek khanate. The word "kazak" is Turkish for "free person," and once they got free of their Mongol overlords, the Kazaks established themselves east of what is now Uzbekistan along the northern branch of the Tienshan Mountains, and I'm pleased to report they're still here.

After one last nightcap, I got up to lower the flap of our yurt just as the moon was rising over a nearby peak. It wasn't that we didn't want moonlight inside our yurt, it was the witch we were worried about. The Kazaks say she lives on the moon and eats human hearts. She is the one with the bent back and the bag of sand. Nobody knows exactly when she developed her strange addiction, but when the Moon God found out, he was very upset. He enjoyed a high reputation among earthlings, and he didn't want to lose it, so he gave the old crone a bag of sand and told her she couldn't come to Earth again until she counted every grain

Kazak hosts at Lake of Heaven

in the bag. And so she started counting. But every time she gets near the bottom, the Moon God sends swallows to swoop down and scatter all the sand, and she has to start counting again. I looked at the moon just long enough to make sure she was still there, then lowered the flap of our yurt and went to sleep on a hill that overlooked Heaven Lake.

The lake was formed long ago by landslides that blocked the only side not hemmed in by the Tienshan Mountains. Then, five years before we visited, the Chinese built a road to the lake, and it was now a tourist destination. Despite the daily arrival of a few hundred day-trippers, the slopes around the lake still belong to the Kazaks, who have been grazing their sheep here during the summer for hundreds, if not thousands, of years. The grazing rights around the lake were shared by five extended families, and to supplement their income they started renting out yurts to the handful of visitors who stayed past sundown. The fee was a modest 10RMB, or $2, per night. They also took visitors on horseback rides for ten bucks a day. That sounded like a good idea, and Finn and I went to sleep dreaming of life on horseback with the wind blowing in our beards.

Finn with Kazak guide

The next morning, just after breakfast, our hosts saddled up three ponies, two for us and one for our guide, and we started down the road that continued along the south side of the lake another kilometer or so. Unfortunately, the mayor of Urumchi was also visiting that day, and the road was blocked. No problem on a horse. Our horses climbed across a ridge, and we soon found ourselves beyond the mayor and his entourage in a wilderness of fir trees and meadows, with the occasional patch of dandelions and the odd tin can or two.

It took us ninety minutes to reach the far end of the lake and another hour to reach the corral where riders dismounted and continued into the mountains on foot, which was what we did. The trail branched off to the base camp of one of the highest peaks in the Tienshan Range: Bogda Peak. In the distance, we could see its 5,400-meter summit. It was too far for the likes of us, and we were quite content to find a place to sit beside the stream that tumbled out of the mountains and that filled the lake with the elixir of Heaven.

Mountain stream and Bogda Peak

It took us two and a half hours to get there on horseback and foot, and we were in no hurry to leave. After traveling along the Silk Road, to find ourselves beside a rushing stream just below the snowline surrounded by fir trees and grass meadows was as unexpected as it was welcome. After about an hour, our guide broke the news that if we delayed any longer, we would be riding home in the dark. And so we returned to our mounts and headed back down the trail. Apparently there was some sort of competition going on among our horses, and our guide occasionally had to lift his switch or give a low, almost inaudible whistle to bring them back in line. They were amazing mounts. They waded across rock-strewn streams and sauntered across log bridges as if the word stumble didn't exist. I had never seen such sure-footed animals. The horse is a Kazak's most important possession, and after years of training they develop an unusually close relationship. After a Kazak dies, no one is allowed to ride his horse.

Altogether, we spent five hours in the saddle that day. Afterwards, when we tried to sit down in our yurt, we realized we would never be cowboys. Walking at least took our minds off our butts, so we ambled down the road to the parking lot and the Tienchih Restaurant, where we had eaten following our arrival the previous day. It was the premier joint on the mountain. Previous visitors left their comments in the restaurant's journal, like this brief accolade: "Very delicious food. Why doesn't the state own this restaurant." Signed "Mao Ts'e-tung."

After another dreamy night beneath the moon, our Kazak hosts woke us, built a fire in our stove, and brought us some fresh mare's milk. We then walked outside and watched the morning mist lift its veil from the lake. We asked our hosts why no one was fishing. They said there were several species of trout but no one was allowed to catch them ever since the lake was declared a nature reserve. The only time they ate fish was when nature reserve officials went out to collect samples. Similar restrictions had also been imposed on hunting wildlife, which included bear, mountain sheep, mule deer, and wolves.

In ancient times, the Kazaks considered wolves the totem of their tribe and called them the gray-bearded warriors. Kazak songs are full of stories about wolves leading their people out of dangers and hard times.

Kazaks still hang wolf bones around their children's necks as talismans, and they're among the few Asians who consider eating dog meat taboo.

Another creature Kazaks venerate is the falcon, and for a most peculiar reason. They think that whenever they do something wrong it's the work of a gremlin sitting on their shoulders, and the only creature that can see these gremlins is the falcon. Hence, Kazaks like to keep a falcon around, not just for hunting small game but for making sure gremlins keep their distance.

Among the Kazaks, even trees come in for veneration, especially lone trees. According to Kazak legends, it was from just such a tree that their ancestors were born a long, long time ago. It's a legend shared by many other tribes, including those in Southwest China such as the Tung.

It was with great reluctance that Finn and I finally said good-bye to the descendants of the tree people, who came out of the forest eons ago to herd woolly sheep in the foothills of the Mountains of Heaven. After two nights in a yurt at Heaven Lake, we returned to Urumchi, which was Persian for "I told you we should have turned right." About the only good thing I can think of to say about Urumchi is thank the Goddess of Mercy there's an airport, and thank her again for saving us two seats on a plane scheduled to leave the next day. And thank her once more for arranging the financial package that made possible the Urumchi Holiday Inn. Yes, the Holiday Inn.

Finn and I never thought we would be glad to see the old innkeeper of the Western World. At $100 a night, the rooms were far too expensive for our budget. But there was more to the Holiday Inn than rooms. There was a bar. And believe it or not, every evening way out here 2,500 kilometers from the sea—farther from the sea than any other city in the world—there's Happy Hour. We looked at the sign as if we had seen a mirage. But it was no mirage. Every evening between six and eight o'clock, beer and wine were purveyed at your standard Happy Hour rate of two for the price of one. And the beer was cold. And the waitresses were dressed in tartan vests, and they knelt down at our table to pour our beers into tall Miller High Life glasses. And they poured it slow, and we slipped a little something into their little vest pockets and watched them smile. And they brought us all the peanuts and raisins and caraway breadsticks we could eat, all of which were free. To think a few hours earlier we were squatting in sheep dung, and now we were lounging in upholstered chairs, drinking icy beer and listening to Mozart coming from the string quartet in the lobby. No way were we on the Silk Road.

Seeing as how we had entered a break in the temporal dimension of the universe, it seemed as good a time as any to write letters home, and our waitress brought us envelopes from the front desk—and the envelopes even had glue on them. This was some kind of place. Speaking of mail: Urumchi was without doubt the finest place from which we ever mailed a package in all of China. Mailing packages in the Middle Kingdom could be a real ordeal demanding a great deal of patience and sewing skill. Until recently, Chinese post offices wouldn't accept any international parcel unless it was sewn up inside something resembling a laundry bag, and it was up to you to go find the material and sew it up yourself. But the winds of reform had begun to blow even at the post office, and nowadays some post offices were beginning to toy with the idea of accepting cardboard boxes and even brown wrapping paper. Apparently, the Urumchi post office was at the leading edge of such reform, which wasn't surprising, considering the number of intellectuals exiled here during the Cultural Revolution.

First of all, the city's main post office was centrally located, within walking distance of our hotel as well as the Holiday Inn bar. Second, just inside the front door there was a counter selling pre-sewn bags, cardboard boxes, wrapping paper, whatever you needed. And third, the staff at the international section not only helped us sew our bags and put bands around our boxes, they even helped us fill out all those forms labeled in French. I take back everything bad I ever said about Urumchi.

After writing letters home, it was time to do a bit of reading. Earlier that day after mailing our package home, we tried to track down a few books about the Uighurs and Kazaks we had been visiting. We visited every bookstore in the city, all three of them, but we couldn't find a single book in Chinese, much less English, about the people who made up the majority of the province's population. "Oh, you want Uighur literature? You'll find it right over there in the Uighur section, assuming you can read Uighur." How, we had to wonder, could the Chinese possibly understand the other ethnic groups with whom they shared the province, if they couldn't read about them?

In the end, I had to settle for a book of poems about Urumchi written by a Chinese official two hundred years ago. I opened it to the section entitled "Folkways." The first poem was about the days when Chinese officials required purveyors of wine to hang blue curtains over their doorways, and all merchants to plant willows in front of their shops:

> *Blue curtains line every willow-shaded street*
> *here in the West people love the land of drink*
> *imagine a hick town where a ladle means you're rich*
> *and your wine bill for the year is two tons of gold*

We were lucky we arrived two hundred years later. That reminded us, we needed to order one more round before Happy Hour ended. And more breadsticks, please.

And so Finn and I sat there drinking two-for-the-price-of-one beers for as long as we could, until finally it was time to settle up and go home—which was just across the street at the Hungshan Hotel. After paying our bill, we sauntered through the lobby, tipped our nonexistent hats to the members of the string quartet and the doormen, and returned to the real world.

Just past the hotel entrance, a Uighur stopped me and asked if I wanted to change money. I was getting a little low on RMB, so I asked him the rate. He said 125 RMB for 100 FEC (Foreign Exchange Certificates, which was the currency all foreigners were forced to use in those days). That was the highest rate we had heard since we began this trip. Up until then the difference had been about 20 percent. Suddenly now it was 25 percent. It was too good to be true, so I jumped on it and offered to change a thousand. The man got out his calculator and came up with the correct figure. Then he reached into his pocket and handed me the RMB. I counted it, and as usual it came out short, so I handed it back to him. Reluctantly, he added the necessary notes. Then he asked to see my FEC. I handed it to him, and he handed me his RMB. Fortunately, all those Happy Hour beers hadn't impaired my vision as much as it had my judgment. I spotted the sleight of hand and grabbed his wrist. Out of his sleeve fell half the RMB I should have received but was about to lose. Somehow I managed to grab back my FEC, made sure it was all there, then threw what was left of his money back in his face. I was mad at myself. Once again, I had made a tactical error. First and last rule in changing money: never take your money out until the other person's money is not only counted but in your pocket. Never, never, never. Especially after Happy Hour.

We stumbled back to our hotel, half pleased and half embarrassed, but we made it back and had just enough energy to pack our bags. We had an early morning date with destiny at the Urumchi airport. It was going to be a big day. We were finally blowing the industrial burg of Urumchi once and for all. We were headed for Yining seven hundred kilometers to the west, just inside China's border with Kazakhstan. The bus took two days to get there, but the plane only needed ninety minutes. Obviously, the plane was the way to go, but tickets weren't always available, and the plane didn't always fly. Fortunately, we managed to get reservations the day we arrived in Urumchi, but we weren't allowed to actually buy our tickets until the day before we were scheduled to leave and only after the airport called to confirm that the plane was ready. Fortunately, it was, and so were we. We got up at five-thirty the next morning and woke up the hotel doorman, who woke up the floor attendant, who made sure we didn't steal any towels. Only then were we allowed to proceed to the airport bus waiting a few blocks away at the airline ticket office. It left right on time at six-thirty and only took twenty minutes to get to the airport, where we suddenly found ourselves with two hours to twiddle our thumbs. We twiddled until nine o'clock, when our flight was finally announced, and filed out the door past the security guards and started walking toward a Boeing 737 parked on the runway. One of the guards yelled at us and pointed in the other direction. Our plane turned out to be an Ilyushin 224 turboprop, and it was parked just outside the maintenance hangar. Not a good sign. But we were so happy to be leaving Urumchi, what the hell? We were feeling lucky. We walked over and climbed up the ramp and joined thirty other lucky souls.

The stewardess standing in the doorway confirmed that the plane was, indeed, bound for Yining. We found our seats and waited for the plane to take off. Yining was only ninety minutes away. But first we had to make it over a spur of the Tienshan Mountains and the 5,500-meter summit of Mount Polokenu. I had been flying in airplanes for forty-five years, but as we left Urumchi behind and approached Mount Polokenu we came as close as I had ever been to a mountain without walking on it. There we were nearing the end of the twentieth century, and we were still flying by the seat of our pants. I couldn't help but think back to the stories my mother told me about the early days of commercial aviation. Sixty years earlier, she was a member of American Airlines' first graduating class of stewardesses. In those days, you needed more than a pretty face to qualify. Stewardesses also had to be registered nurses. Air travel wasn't just another means of transportation, it was an adventure, and only the very wealthy, the very-much-in-a-hurry, and the very crazy flew.

According to my mother, at least once a month planes landed somewhere other than the airport. Sometimes it was to avoid bad weather, sometimes to get gas, or sometimes just to find out where the Hell they were. At least we knew where we were, although we weren't sure why we were there. We were about three hundred meters above the 5,500-meter summit of Mount Polokenu. The drone from the propellers of our Ilyushin 224 muffled the gasps of our fellow passengers, who, like us, were wondering what we were doing flying low enough to see the crystalline dust rising from an avalanche.

Mount Polokenu was the final snowy gesture of the northernmost branch of the Tienshan Mountains that divide the Junggar Basin north of Urumchi from the Ili Valley to the west. Apparently, the pilot was taking advantage of the perfect weather to save fuel, and he came sufficiently close for everyone to get out their prayer beads. The gods must have been just outside the window. With their help, we passed safely over Polokenu's jagged, snowcapped peak and began our gradual descent across a huge plateau dotted with the white yurts of Kazak herders. They looked like mushrooms—the yurts, not the herders—although we could see them too, we were that low. A few minutes later, the plateau split apart, and we followed the Ili River west to Yining, our next oasis on the Silk Road.

伊寧

13. Yining

BACK IN THE THIRD CENTURY BC, the Ili Valley became the refuge of several nomadic groups forced by the Huns to abandon the grasslands of the Kansu Corridor. Among these were the Wusun, and it was this tribe the Chinese ambassador Chang Ch'ien approached about establishing an alliance against those who drove them from their homelands. The alliance never worked out, but the Chinese continued to make forays into the Ili Valley from time to time, most recently in the eighteenth century to counter Russian influence in the area. Here we

Finn and author at China-Kazakhstan border market

were 250 years later, landing at the Yining airport in a Russian-built plane and being welcomed inside the airport terminal by an announcer speaking Russian.

Yining was just east of the former Soviet Union and the newly independent Republic of Kazakhstan. Unfortunately, we arrived on a Saturday, and it didn't take long to learn that weekends are not a good time to visit this outpost of the Middle Kingdom. During our travels through China, we had yet to make a hotel reservation, and we didn't need to. If the first hotel was full, there was always room at old number two. In Yining, we finally found a spartan cell at old number four. The problem with hotel rooms in Yining was that the city is less than two hours by bus from the border, and on weekends the place is mobbed by members of the Russian and Kazak proletariat doing a little trading on the side. Up until then our travels along the Silk Road had taken us through areas whose populations consisted of Uighurs and Han Chinese and a few Kazaks down from the grasslands. Suddenly we were walking down the street past dozens of blue-eyed, red-haired Russians. All we could do was stare. It was hard to believe we were still in China. But like us, the Russians we saw were just passing through.

Most of the Russians living in Yining when the Chinese took over Hsinchiang joined their relatives on the other side of the border. Life under Stalin was somehow preferable to life under Mao. Who was to say who got the better deal? Still, not all Russians left. Several thousand decided to stay, and they made up one of the oddest communities in China. Imagine a place in China where people celebrated Christmas, with Christmas trees, and Christmas carols. And they celebrated for three whole days, or until the vodka ran out.

The several thousand Russians living on the Chinese side of the border are known as Elossu. They are members of the Eastern Orthodox Church that split off from the Catholic Church a thousand years ago, and it is their religion that led them here in the first place. In the eighteenth and nineteenth centuries, a reformist branch of the Orthodox Church gained the upper hand at the Russian court and began persecuting Christians who insisted on clinging to the old ways. Among those who refused to change and who fled into China were the ancestors of Yining's Russian community, which numbered nearly 10,000 at the time of our visit. They still fasted on Wednesday to atone for the sins of Judas, and they fasted on Friday as well to share the sufferings of Christ, and they celebrated Christmas on January 7.

In addition to the city's Russian community, another group whose ancestors came from the other side of the border were the Tatars. The Tatars share the same roots as the Russians and other Slavic groups of Central Asia. But the Tatars give those roots a few unique twists. For example, they honor Muhammad, not Jesus, as the fountainhead of their religion, and they trace their ancestry back to the hordes of Genghis Khan, instead of the Great Slav. And if pressed, they can trace their ancestry back even further to an old she-wolf. Even today, the Tatars like to hang the bone of a wolf's hind leg around their necks to ward off evil spirits. And during Tatar festivals, old women dress up like wolves, and every once in a while children who have been bad are said to disappear.

The first thing Finn and I decided to do after we recovered from our flight and our first night in the dingiest of hotels was to visit the border that made all this possible. Every day one of the travel services in Yining organizes a trip to the market just inside the Chinese side of the border. And so we joined twenty other visitors from all parts of China curious to see what was being traded. Two hours and a lunch stop later, we found out.

The market was inside a huge warehouse in the middle of a vacant field a kilometer from the border. A large burly man stopped us at the door and said we had to pay to get in. Pay to get in a market? That was a first. Since this was why we were here, we acquiesced and paid the 10RMB entry fee and walked inside. The place was full of Chinese selling clothes and Russians buying clothes. According to our guide, the Russians usually arrived in the morning and sold binoculars, watches, leather boots, and other products of light industry. Then, with the money they made, they bought Chinese-made clothes to sell in Russia. Down jackets were popular items. We spent about five minutes struggling through the crush of bodies and garments before we finally gave up and walked back outside. It wasn't what we had envisioned.

After about an hour, once all the members of our tour had satisfied their buying frenzy, we proceeded to the nearby border checkpoint for a photo opportunity. The place was called Korgas, and it was hyped as the major entrepôt on China's border with Kazakhstan. It wasn't exactly the Berlin Wall, but we took the required photo and headed back to Yining. Our tour, though, wasn't over.

After driving twenty kilometers back toward Yining, we turned off on a side road that led to the blue-tiled Persian-style tomb of Telug Timur. Telug Timur was a descendant of Genghis Khan. And from his Mongol ancestors, he inherited a kingdom that included the Ili Valley. Telug Timur was an active ruler, and an inquisitive one. Before his death in 1364, he became the first Mongol ruler to be converted to Islam, and he insisted his subjects follow suit. Among those subjects was a young man named Tamerlane who was so impressed by his master's new faith that he took it upon himself to try to convert all of Asia, which he very

Tomb of Telug Timur

Drum tower built by Lin Tse-hsu in Huiyuan

nearly did. By the time he died in 1405, Tamerlane extended the Timurid Empire, as it was called, to include all of Iran, Iraq, Afghanistan, Georgia, South Carolina, and Armenia. His armies also devastated large parts of Syria, Eastern Turkey, Northern India, and Southern Russia. As he was planning to invade China, Tamerlane suddenly died, and his heir turned out to be more interested in the peaceful conversion of infidels, which was fortunate for the Chinese. In any case, between Telug Timur, Tamerlane, and their successors, the spread of Islam began in earnest in this part of Asia, and it is largely due to their pioneering efforts that Islam is still the Silk Road's dominant faith.

In addition to stopping to visit Telug Timur's mausoleum, our tour also stopped in the town of Huiyuan, which was once the political and administrative center in this part of Hsinchiang, not Yining. In the middle of the old part of town, we stopped to visit a drum tower built in the middle of the nineteenth century by Commissioner Lin. Poor Commissioner Lin, a man ahead of his time.

Lin's full name was Lin Tse-hsu. In December 1838, he was appointed High Commissioner in charge of carrying out the emperor's anti-opium policy in the Kuangchou area. Following his arrival in the spring of 1839, Lin issued an ultimatum to the foreign merchants there that they would not be allowed to leave until they had surrendered all the opium in their possession, and to this indignity they were forced to acquiesce.

The trade in opium, though, continued. Incensed by the foreigners' disdain for Chinese laws, Commissioner Lin finally closed Kuangchou permanently to British ships in January of 1840. And he followed this up with a list of rewards for the capture and destruction of British ships as well as the capture and killing of Britons. Naturally, this news was not well received among foreign merchants, and the Opium War ensued— which resulted not only in the embarrassing defeat of Chinese forces but the exile of Commissioner Lin to the farthest possible post in the empire, which happened to be the town of Huiyuan, where we stopped to visit the drum tower he built following his arrival in 1843. Doubtlessly, it was Lin's way of reminding people of his unjust fate.

His exile, however, only succeeded in making him a national hero. In coming years, I suspect foreigners will be hearing Commissioner Lin's name again during trade negotiations. In addition to taking the lead in resisting British imperialists to the south, Lin also sounded a warning regarding the Russians to the north. Lin's fears were not without basis. In 1871, the Tsar's forces invaded the Ili Valley under the pretense of protecting itself from a rebellion on the other side of the Tienshan Mountains. Ten years later, Moscow forced Beijing to cede part of the valley, and Beijing is still upset about this loss of territory it had itself acquired only two hundred years earlier. We also visited the compound where Lin stayed during his exile, but other than two stone lions, there wasn't much to see. The biggest find for us was two cold beers at a store opposite the drum tower. Apparently the Elossu influence. At least we returned to Yining with our thirst quenched.

After our tour ended, we realized we were once again running low on RMB. While we were walking back to our hotel, we stopped to negotiate with some local moneychangers. I was out of FEC, but I still had a couple Ben Franklins and asked about the rate for $100. I was surprised to hear it was 700, which was 5 percent higher than the usual black market rate. Once again I pounced on it, and once again I witnessed a new twist on that blackest of markets.

Normally, when a moneychanger offers an unusually high rate, especially without lengthy negotiations, the buyer should beware. But we were almost out of RMB and heading into territory where anything else likely wouldn't be recognized as legal tender. In Urumchi we were recently reminded not to pull out our money until the other person's money was counted and safely in our pocket. This time after pocketing the 700RMB, I handed the moneychanger my Ben Franklin, and he called over his partner. His partner held the $100 note up to the light then rolled it up and proceeded to rub it with his hands, as if he were trying to see if the ink would come off. Sure enough, the man showed us some ink on his hands and returned the note, claiming it was counterfeit, and he asked me to return the 700RMB he had already given me. As he handed me back the rolled-up bill, I reached into my pocket for his money, then I stopped. The bill he was handing me didn't look like the same bill I handed him. Sure enough, it was a $1 bill. I suggested that if he really thought it was counterfeit we should seek the services of the nearest policeman, and his money stayed in my pocket. Once again, I escaped by the skin of my teeth.

In recent years, the Yining area had attracted thousands of Han Chinese, lured here by the opening up of cross-border trade with the Kazak Republic less than a hundred kilometers to the west. But the majority of the area's population still consisted of Uighurs and Kazaks and a few smaller ethnic groups, like the Hsipos.

The Hsipos' homeland was originally thousands of kilometers to the east, in the same general area of Northeast China where the Manchus lived. Not long after the Manchus conquered China and established the Ch'ing dynasty in the seventeenth century, they sent 3,000 Hsipos to the Ili Valley to guard the empire's new northwest frontier. After six years, the Hsipos petitioned the Manchu emperor to let them return home, and he responded by extending their term of duty another sixty years, and they have been here ever since. Over the past two hundred years, their numbers have increased to 30,000, and most of them live twenty kilometers southwest of Yining in Chapchal County—which was where they settled when they first came here in 1764. Before they were conscripted into the Manchu army, the Hsipos lived by hunting and fishing. But when they arrived in the Ili Valley, they were forced to support themselves by farming. Still, they have managed to maintain a number of their ancient skills, and every year on the eighteenth day of the fourth lunar month they hold archery and wrestling contests to commemorate the day their ancestors set off on a trek that took them seventeen months—and which most of them didn't complete. The Hsipo celebration, though, doesn't hold a candle to a similar gathering held by the Mongols every year at a place called Bayanbulak, and Bayanbulak just happened to be on the way to Kucha, which was our next stop on the Silk Road.

We had heard that foreigners weren't allowed to travel the road to Kucha across the Bayanbulak Plateau. But we didn't want to go back to

Urumchi, by bus or by plane—and we decided, why not try the Kucha road? As luck would have it, a visit to the local bus station turned up two tickets on the daily Kucha Express. Normally, the price for bus tickets in China is the same for everyone, but this time the stationmaster insisted we pay double. She laughed when we showed her our teacher IDs.

When I asked the stationmaster what was the reasoning behind the extra charge, without pausing to make up an excuse, she said everyone knew that when Chinese traveled abroad they were charged double, so naturally it was only fair for the Chinese to charge foreigners double when they traveled in China. I asked her where she had heard this news about Chinese being charged double in foreign countries. Again, without pausing, she said that was what the government told everyone. Ah, yes, the government, that bastion of truth in an unfair world. Of course, our protestations that such was not the case had no effect on her. She just shook her head and said the government would never lie to the people. We suggested the government had been misinformed. But it was a moot point. We were glad to pay whatever it cost to avoid the two-day bus ride back to Urumchi, much less another hair-raising flight.

巴音布魯克

14. Bayanbulak

T HE NEXT MORNING WE BOARDED the daily bus to Kucha. It
was a two-day ride, but it was still the quickest way for us to get
there. We left in the rain and settled in for a long day. Once we were
out of Yining, the bus wound its way between the barren foothills of
the Tienshan Mountains to the south and the banks of the Ili River to
the north. The landscape on the other side of the river was a vast plain
with few settlements. For the next several hours, we saw more camels
than people.

Naturally, our bus broke down. It wasn't the ideal place to experience mechanical problems, but at least we were able to snooze while our driver improvised a solution to whatever it was that ailed the engine. If it can be fixed, a Chinese bus driver can fix it, and our driver was no exception. After an hour, we resumed our progress into the wilderness, and by late afternoon we reached the isolated intersection where one road leads north to Urumchi and the other leads south to Kucha.

We turned south and immediately began zigzagging our way up an endless series of switchbacks into the fog-shrouded, fir-covered slopes of another branch of the Tienshan Mountains. Along the way we passed a yurt with a string of ponies and a motorcycle parked out front—the motorcycle, no doubt, was for going to town. By the time we reached the summit, my altimeter indicated 2,550 meters, and we were driving through a snowstorm. The summit turned out to be a huge plateau. It was, in fact, the Bayanbulak Plateau. But the county seat of Bayanbulak, which was the only "town" for a hundred kilometers in any direction, was still an hour away.

Eventually, the snow eased up, and eleven hours after leaving Yining we pulled into the bus compound north of town. A few blocks away in the middle of town we could see the façade of a movie theater. It was the only building that wasn't huddling against the ground for warmth. Despite the lure of entertainment, we made our first order of business checking into the best room in the bus compound. For 40RMB, or about $8, we got two beds, a ton of blankets, a desk, a couple of chairs, and a coal stove—an asset that would later prove more of a disadvantage, but more on that later.

After putting on our silk long johns—without which we never travel in China—we moseyed down to the theater. While we were moseying, two women came riding down the street after jumping a stream on their coal-black ponies. They wore their hair long, and they were wrapped in so many layers of clothes, if it hadn't been for their hair we wouldn't have guessed they were women. It turned out Bayanbulak is in the middle of the biggest Mongol region outside Inner or Outer Mongolia.

Bayanbulak Plateau

Bayanbulak Plateau trading post and mosque

Bayanbulak is basically a trading post, a place where herders come to trade sheepskins for manufactured goods, things like thermoses and tea kettles and woks. Finn and I wondered what sort of things were for sale, but we weren't in the market for a wok or a thermos. We poked our heads through a doorway of a store that sold coats, and the woman inside asked us what we wanted. There were still snowflakes in the air, and Finn was feeling a bit cold, so we asked her if she had any really heavy coats. The lady said she didn't have any in the store, but she had two at home. We followed her to the edge of town, which was only four blocks away, to her mud-walled two-room house.

Apparently the clothing business was good. She had a small color TV, a big radio–cassette player, and a small, battery-operated piano. From her bedroom-cum-storage room she came out with what Finn was look-ing for: a huge olive-green army-style coat with a whole sheep inside. The price, she said, was 220RMB, or less than $40. It was perfect. Guar-anteed to keep anyone warm in the coldest weather. Thus equipped, we moseyed back to the bus compound and the heat of our coal stove. The theater, it turned out, wasn't open.

I had never heard of Bayanbulak before. But the man who took care of the bus compound filled us in when we arrived. The place attracts thousands of people from all over the world who come here to see what might be called the Mongol Olympics. In addition to the standard wrestling and archery and horseback contests, the Mongols have a wonderful time playing soccer on horseback using a sheep carcass for the ball. The contests are held just outside of town, and somehow all the visitors find a place to stay, even if it's underneath the stars. There weren't any hotels, just a couple dozen rooms at the bus compound—where we were glad to be spending the night, with a stove in our room.

In fact, we had the only stove in the bus compound, and our fellow passengers took turns coming into our room and warming themselves against the cold. It was snowing when we arrived, but with nightfall the sky turned out to be full of stars. We left the warmth of our room briefly for a dinner in the bus compound "restaurant," which served everyone the same food: mutton and potatoes. Afterwards, we made one final trip to the great outdoors then returned to our room and opened our last bottle of wine. It was the cabernet called Pearl of the Silk Road. Halfway through the bottle, we received one last contingent of visitors. This time it was a group of six young men, all of them sporting gold rings with big red stones.

We offered them some wine, and they tried it, but they almost spit it out. Dry wines, we gathered, don't have much of a future on the Silk Road. Then it was their turn. Out came the matches and tinfoil, and they asked us if we'd like to "chase the dragon." We held onto our wineglasses out of self-defense and declined. Still, they weren't about to leave, and we had no choice but to hear all about the newest trade good on the Silk Road: heroin. It came up from Burma, they said, via Yunnan, then traveled through Szechuan and Kansu, and finally through Hsinchiang to Yining, where it crossed the border into Kazakhstan. Its final destination, they said, was Moscow—which had become one of Asia's biggest markets for "China White." The Russian rings the boys were sporting were their cut of the action, and they were heading back to Kucha to turn their baubles into more capital to buy more heroin. All we could say was, "Good night sweet princes."

And so we spent the night in the trading post of Bayanbulak high on the Bayanbulak Plateau. The elevation was over 2,500 meters, and the surrounding snowcapped ridges were twice that. The plateau is the summer home of a branch of the Mongols known as the Torgut who migrated here in the eighteenth century to escape the expansionist policies of the Tsar. It was a wild, desolate-looking landscape, and the only movement we saw during our hour or two outside before sunset were a few riders coming down from the mountains to trade animal skins for provisions. Tens of thousands of Mongols converge on the place at the beginning of August for the Mongol Olympics and Trade Fair. But it was the end of September when we arrived.

We also arrived too late to see the swans. If it had been spring or summer, we could have hired a couple of horses and ridden out to the Bayanbulak Swan Reserve. The reserve was established in 1980 and encompasses an area of 100,000 hectares that includes Swan Lake and its surrounding marshland. The lake is ten kilometers long and thirty kilometers across and is home to seventy-two kinds of migratory birds, the most prominent of which were three species of swans.

But the swans were long gone. Outside our room a few snowflakes were swirling among the stars, and half a dozen fellow passengers were warming their hands around our stove wondering why we preferred sipping red wine to inhaling heroin fumes. Apparently, heroin was sufficiently new to the Silk Road to enjoy an undeservedly harmless reputation. As they headed back to their unheated rooms, we finished our wine and went to sleep. Sometime during the night, I thought I heard a wolf howl.

Nearly 50,000 Mongols still live their traditional way of life on the plateau, hundreds of kilometers from anything that could be called a town. Like all Mongols, they trace their ancestry back to the beginning of the Earth. Long before any humans were on the planet, a fairy maiden flew down one day from the sky to bathe in the cool waters of a lake high in the grasslands of Central Asia. It was a lake not unlike Swan Lake, where the wild swans fly down from the sky every spring and spend their summers, and where the Torguts herd their sheep and let their horses run wild.

Mongol horseman on the Bayanbulak Plateau

Meanwhile, following her bath, the fairy sat down on a rock to dry off her wings. Although she was a fairy, she was still a female of the species, and it just happened to be her period. When she flew off, she left behind a few drops of blood on the rock. Not long afterwards, an ape came along and urinated on the same spot. Then, he too left. And the fairy blood and the ape urine mixed, and the seasons passed, and after 9,999 years, the mixture produced the first human being, who was half-fairy and half-ape and a hundred percent Mongol.

We could have slept forever in Torgutland. But we didn't have forever. At five o'clock our alarm went off. Our bus was due to leave in thirty minutes. Our coal stove went out during the night, so we stayed under our blankets as long as possible. Finally, we heard the bus driver turn on his engine. We put on our clothes and shoes—we slept in our long johns, grabbed our packs, and walked outside to reclaim our seats. The bus was right outside the bus compound door, and the driver was ready to go. A few minutes later, we were rolling again. No sign of the sun, just a Cheshire cat moon smiling at Orion. When we asked the bus driver why we were leaving so early, he said he couldn't make it over the pass unless he got there before the sun came up and turned the road to glass.

As we pulled out of the compound, one of the boys who had visited our room the night before stood up and held up a bottle. He said, "I have the foreigner's wine." Then he took a chug. Finn and I had emptied it before we went to sleep. But we had filled it back up during the night. The boy's euphoria was brief. He tried to reach the bus door, but he didn't make it that far. Finn and I cringed. What could we say?

Everyone on board laughed, while the boy vomited in the doorwell. Then everyone went back to shivering—everyone except me and Finn. Me, I had on my silk long johns. And Finn was wearing an entire sheep. While we rolled across the Bayanbulak Plateau in the predawn blackness, the boy returned to his seat and tried to open a window. Unfortunately, the windows were all frozen shut. Then he went back and stood in the doorwell.

As we rattled through the darkness, we imagined wolves roaming outside waiting for our bus to break down, and I remembered this story

I read several years ago by a Manchu writer about a Mongol hunter and a wolf. It was a long story, but we had a long way to go, and dawn was another hour away. Still, I'll skip the beginning and get right to the heart of this one.

One day a Mongol hunter was working his way through a birch forest. Nothing, not even rabbit tracks. Not a good day for the Mongol hunter. Finally, as he was walking out of the woods, he stopped, threw himself onto the ground, and rolled back into the trees. From behind the snowdrifts that surrounded the edge of the forest, he watched an ancient spectacle: on a nearby hill eighteen wolves were standing, as if they were frozen stiff. It was February, the mating season. But among the wolves of the high grasslands, only one she-wolf in every pack can bear cubs: the queen. This year, as every year, the queen had a challenger, and two of the wolves began to tense for the fight. Even their hair seemed to have muscles. Suddenly the hill exploded into a whirlwind of snow and blood, and the snow plain echoed with the snarls and cries of two she-wolves battling for the right to motherhood.

That spring, the old queen was deposed and limped away. Meanwhile, the male wolves licked the wounds of the winner, and the pack moved on, leaving the loser to fend for herself. From behind his cover in a nearby birch forest, the Mongol hunter breathed easier. He had a hunting rifle. A rifle was useless against a pack of wolves. A lone wolf, though, was another matter. As the old she-wolf limped down the hill in his direction, the Mongol hunter lifted his rifle to his shoulder.

Suddenly the wolf stopped, sniffed the air and changed directions. Ever so slowly she moved closer to a small pile of snow, unaware that a steel barrel was pointed straight at her. Suddenly the Mongol hunter realized there was something alive under that pile of snow, and if he shot and missed the wolf, he would hit whatever it was. And he knew what it was. There was no time to think, only act. He grabbed a birch branch and broke it. The snap echoed across the snow plain, and the wolf stopped just long enough to see the Mongol hunter standing up and pointing his rifle at it. Instead of tearing into the pile of snow, the she-wolf bolted away and disappeared into a grove of elm trees.

The Mongol hunter lowered his rife and walked over to the snow pile. He looked up just once to make sure the wolf was gone, then he started digging through the snow. He didn't have to dig far. After a few seconds, he pulled out a man holding a handful of rocks he had picked up in the foolish hope that they would help him defend himself against the pack of wolves. The man was obviously an outsider. He was wearing a new leather coat and a padded vest and new leather boots but no wool socks. And he was frozen stiff, as if he had been carved out of wood.

The Mongol hunter rolled the frozen man over and put the back of his hand against the man's nose. He could feel breath. The man was still alive. But he wouldn't be alive long if the hunter didn't act. He took off his belt and hung it around his neck, then with his knife he cut off the man's frozen coat. From the lining of the man's vest, thousands of hundred-RMB notes fluttered across the snow. The Mongol hunter didn't know what to think, but he didn't have time to think. He gathered up the notes and stuffed them into the man's plastic bag then went to work with his belt. He flayed the frozen man as if he had gone mad. Within minutes, the man was a mass of bleeding welts. Finally, the frozen man opened his eyes. The man was conscious, but the hunter didn't stop. Now he began whipping the man's feet. The man rolled away and lurched to his feet and started running—or trying to run. The Mongol hunter gathered up his rifle and the man's belongings and drove him like a sheep, first one way, then the other, making him move, making him sweat. Finally, he drove him into an empty hut the local hunters used when they had to spend a night on the plain. While the man cowered in a corner, the Mongol hunter started a fire and took a swig from a bottle of white lightning left behind by a previous hunter. He offered it to the man, then he realized he knew him.

The man was a Han Chinese from Kiangsu province who came to the plains several months earlier to make his fortune. The fortune and the tool of his trade were in the plastic bag the Mongol hunter threw at the man's feet. The bag contained 20,000RMB and a Seagull camera. The man's modus operandi was to take pictures of herding families and promise to send them their pictures—for a price. But he had been using an empty camera. There was no film in the bag. The Mongol hunter and his family were among those he duped, and he vowed to deal with the man from Kiangsu in the morning. Then he drifted off to sleep.

Sometime during the night a wolf howled, and the next morning the Mongol hunter found himself alone. He grabbed his rifle and headed off in pursuit of the man who made his family put on their best clothes so he could cheat them. The Mongol hunter had no trouble finding the man's trail, but he saw that there was a second set of footprints. It belonged to the same she-wolf that was about to attack the man before the Mongol hunter chased her off. But there was something strange about the wolf tracks. Instead of four footprints, there were only three. He remembered the howl in the night. Apparently, the wolf had stepped into a trap, and to get loose it had chewed off its own foot.

Just as the Mongol hunter came over a ridge, he saw the man in the gully below. He also spotted the wolf crouching behind some bushes getting ready to attack. The Mongol hunter aimed his rifle, but the trigger was frozen. He realized the man must have peed in the rifle before sneaking away during the night, but it was too late to do anything about it. Meanwhile, the wolf saw the Mongol hunter and forgot about the man and attacked the hunter instead. The hunter ducked, but one of its claws ripped across his face. Somehow, he managed to grab the wolf from behind, and he rode it like a wild horse into a snowdrift. He dug his hands into the wolf's face and gouged out both of its eyes. Then he broke the wolf's back. When the hunter finally rolled free, the man was gone, and once again he took off after him. He was going to kill him for peeing in his rifle.

The hunter knew the direction the man was traveling, and he took a shortcut. When he arrived where he expected the man to pass by, he hid behind a tree. While he waited, he knocked out the last bit of ice from his rifle and made sure there was a shell in the chamber. He didn't have to wait long. As the man came stumbling out of the woods onto the snow plain, the hunter raised his rifle and took aim. But just then the man stopped and raised his hands and cried out. He wasn't crying out to the hunter. He didn't know the hunter was there. The man dropped to his knees and

Telemet Pass

cried out for mercy. He begged for forgiveness. His cries echoed across the snow plain. The Mongol hunter's resolve suddenly waned and vanished. The snow plain had forgiven the man. How else could the hunter explain the man's survival in a world where he didn't belong? He lowered his rifle and turned away and walked back to the hut where the two men had spent the night. While he was gathering his things, he noticed the man's plastic bag. He opened it but couldn't believe his eyes. Inside was the 20,000RMB the man had cheated out of the Mongol herders. The man was giving it back. The Mongol hunter picked up the bag and headed home just as the sun came streaming in the bus window.

A few minutes later, we left the Bayanbulak Plateau and began following a stream into the Telemet Mountains and started climbing. When we set out from the bus compound, my altimeter read 2,500 meters. By the time we reached the pass an hour later, it was 3,100 meters. The pass was actually a long tunnel several hundred meters below the real pass. When we came out the other side the bus driver stopped to change a tire, and we all filed out to answer the call of nature and to warm our hands in the guardhouse, where someone had a coal stove going. Just about

Group photo while driver changes tires at Big Dragon Lake

the time feeling began to return to our toes, we piled back onto the bus and began our descent. Once again we followed a stream, but this time downhill. After an hour, we passed a lake—Big Dragon Lake, to be exact. Fish were rising to the surface in the early morning light, and the shore was lined with reeds. It was a beautiful setting, and the driver stopped once more to change tires. We all piled out again and everyone gathered in a meadow for a group photo: the Uighurs and Kazaks, the heroin dealers, and a bunch of old ladies who kept us supplied with apples and goat cheese—a great snack combination—during our two-day bus ride from Yining.

After the new tire was on, we wound our way down an alpine valley and stopped for lunch at a checkpoint where the stream hit the flatlands and where we suddenly found ourselves driving through one of the most stunning landscapes in China. Except for the occasional fringe of yellow poplars, it was red and completely barren. It looked like the bones of the Earth uncovered at last. The Chinese call the place Chihshashan, or Cinnabar Hills. It was surreal. But so was everything else about our trip from Yining.

庫車

15. Kucha

FINALLY, TWO DAYS AFTER SETTING OUT from China's border with Kazakhstan, we arrived in Kucha. In terms of actual-on-the-road-time, it took us eleven hours to get from Yining to the Mongol trading post of Bayanbulak, then another nine to get to Kucha. That was twenty hours on a bus. Normally twenty hours on a bus required hospitalization afterwards. But this was without doubt the best twenty hours we spent on any mode of transport in China. There was almost no traffic, the driver didn't honk his horn even once, our fellow passengers were all Uighurs and Kazaks—and a colorful and friendly bunch they were indeed, and the scenery was spectacular—especially the last part through the Chihsha, or Cinnabar, Hills. If a photographer wanted to do something special with black and white in China, it would be hard to find a better place. Everybody in China photographs scenic wonders like Huangshan. The Chihsha Hills were virgin territory. But all we could do was watch the spectacle pass by from our bus window.

And so we rolled into Kucha and returned once more to the main branch of the Silk Road, which we left in Turfan to explore the side branch that passed through Urumchi and Yining. From Turfan the main branch continues to Korla, then Kucha. I don't know what we missed in Korla, but in her book on the Silk Road, Judy Bonavia had this to say about it: "There are no historical sites worthy of note apart from Iron Gate Pass, of which only a pile of bricks remains." We presumed we could do better than a pile of bricks in Kucha.

Chihsha Hills

Kucha was one of the most ancient of all Silk Road oases. Exactly how ancient is a matter archaeologists haven't quite worked out. When the Chinese first extended their influence along the Silk Road in the second century BC, Kucha was the capital of the largest of the thirty-six kingdoms on the road between China and India. Its city wall extended for eight kilometers, and people can still visit sections that date back to the T'ang and even the Han dynasties. Inside the Han dynasty sections, archaeologists have also found earlier remains of human settlement dating back 3,000 years.

Exactly what sort of humans is also a subject of some speculation. The consensus is that they were a branch of the Indo-European tribe of Man. One thing for sure is that the people of Kucha loved to sing and dance, and early Chinese visitors were suitably impressed—so impressed, in fact, that the music of Kucha became the most popular form of music in China during the T'ang. Can you imagine Chinese music without the p'i-p'a or the long flute known as the hsiao? Both instruments were introduced to the Chinese from Kucha, along with a whole new way of dressing and dancing. The music and dance scenes in the Buddhist caves of Tunhuang and other Silk Road towns were based mostly on Kuchan models and give a good idea of how sensual the people of this ancient oasis were.

As we stepped out of the bus we had become part of for the past two days, the bus driver yelled to a cart driver that we were old friends and not to overcharge us. And off we went by donkey to our own modest oasis—the Kucha Hotel. There was a fancy new hotel going up on the highway not far from where we got off the bus, but the Kucha Hotel was more our speed: quiet, unpretentious, and with a restaurant that not only stocked cold beer but also Chinese brandy at 10RMB, or $2, a bottle.

While we were enjoying a hot meal and a cold beverage, we met the head of the local foreign affairs office, who was also availing himself of the restaurant's lunchtime cuisine. When we told him we had arrived in Kucha via the Bayanbulak Plateau, he told us we had broken the law. The road was closed to foreigners without permits and a guide. We thanked him for this information and promised never to break the law again. Then we ordered another beer.

Despite finding ourselves in a minor paradise, we didn't linger over our brews long. It was still early in the afternoon, and we wanted to see a few of Kucha's sights, which were not many but were interesting. We began just down the road from our hotel, at the tomb of the "pigeon-killer." The man's name was Molena Ashadin, and he was an Arab missionary who arrived in Kucha 1,300 years ago. One day the man killed a pigeon, and the next day he dropped dead. For some reason his disciples thought this was auspicious and built a shrine that still contains his tomb.

Since there wasn't much else to see near the hotel, we proceeded on foot into the old part of town, where we found the Kucha Mosque—

Kucha's main mosque

supposedly the second-largest mosque in the province. The façade was impressive, but we found village life in the maze of alleyways behind it more interesting. Kucha's weekly bazaar was also supposed to be worth seeing, but it took place on Fridays, and this wasn't a Friday. Other than the remains of the city's ancient wall, there wasn't much else to see. As the afternoon turned to dusk, we returned to our hotel and enjoyed a hot bath and real beds. Kucha may have lost its ancient status, but it was still an oasis.

The next morning we decided to venture farther afield, but we needed to hire our own transportation—which turned out to be rather expensive. In Tunhuang or Turfan, a minivan big enough for five passengers cost less than 200RMB per day. In Kucha, a ramshackle jeep hired through the good offices of the foreign affairs administration cost us 350RMB. The only problem with trying to arrange transport elsewhere was that there didn't seem to be a surplus of idle vehicles in town. And so we paid what we had to and headed for our last set of ruins and our last set of Buddhist caves.

Our tour began with the ruins of Subashi, about twenty kilometers to the northeast. The ruins extend along both sides of the Kucha River, which flows out of the nearby Kizil Mountains. The two shores are a kilometer apart, and during the winter it's possible to walk across. We arrived in fall and had to content ourselves with the only side accessible by jeep.

Subashi wasn't so much a city as it was a Buddhist religious center, and the ruins include the remains of dozens of shrine halls and pagodas and stupas and monk cells. Before it was destroyed in the twelfth century, the name of the complex was Chaohuli. When Hsuan-tsang stopped here in the seventh century on his way to India, one of the things he noted was that male children born of commoners had the backs of their heads flattened by the pressure of a wooden board. When archaeologists recently unearthed a fourth-century tomb at Subashi, its occupant was found to have just such a skull. Unfortunately, the contents of that and other tombs unearthed in the Kucha area were no longer on display. The town's museum had been closed until further notice due to the unexplained disappearance of certain items that now filled the display cases of foreign museums and private collections.

The missing items notwithstanding, the Chaohuli temple complex at Subashi must have been quite a place, especially during the late fourth century when Kucha's most famous resident lived there. We met him earlier in Wuwei and Tunhuang. His name was Kumarajiva, and he is considered one of the two greatest Buddhist translators—the other being Hsuan-Tsang.

Kumarajiva's mother was the sister of the King of Kucha and was named Jiva. She was both beautiful and intelligent, and she refused all suitors, until one day a young Buddhist monk from Kashmir chanced to visit the kingdom. His name was Kumarayana. As soon as Jiva saw Kumarayana, she knew she had found the man she wanted to marry, and she asked her brother to arrange their marriage. The king was happy his sister had finally found someone acceptable and compelled

Ruins of Subashi

Kumarayana to break his vow of chastity and agree to the marriage. The following year Jiva gave birth to a son, Kumarajiva.

When he was seven, Kumarajiva became a monk, and his mother became a nun, and together they traveled to India to study Buddhism from the leading teachers of the day. After he returned to Kucha, Kumarajiva became so well known for his exposition of Buddhist doctrine, his fame spread to China. That was during the early days of Buddhism in China, and the leading Chinese monks were anxious to learn more about their new faith. They asked the emperor to invite Kumarajiva to the capital. It just so happened that the emperor had become somewhat annoyed with the King of Kucha, and he dispatched an army to bring Kumarajiva back to Ch'ang-an so that he could benefit from his instruction.

The year was 382 AD, and the general's name was Lu Kuang. We had already met him in Wuwei. After defeating the King of Kucha, Lu Kuang

Ruins of Subashi

did as ordered and headed back to Ch'ang-an with his prize. But halfway back, he learned that there had been a change in dynasties and decided he would be better off staying where he was. And so Lu Kuang set up his own Silk Road kingdom at Wuwei in the middle of the Kansu Corridor. Kumarajiva stayed in Wuwei for seventeen years, until the new emperor's son finally succeeded in defeating Lu Kuang.

Despite the hardships of his detention, by the time Kumarajiva arrived in Ch'ang-an he was completely fluent in Chinese, and by the time he died twelve years later, he left behind a series of translations that remain among the gems not only of Chinese Buddhism but of Chinese literature as well. South of Sian, there is a small marble stupa in the countryside that contains his ashes, and from the gate of the military police compound in Wuwei, we had viewed the pagoda containing his magic tongue. Now we were in his hometown, but the only evidence that Kumarajiva had ever lived here had long since been scattered by the wind somewhere among the ruins of Subashi.

Next to the ruins of Kaochang and Chiaoho, those of Subashi were the most impressive we had seen on the Silk Road—although we needed a jeep to get there. Since we had hired the vehicle for the day, we continued on. Our next stop was a lone beacon tower that overlooked another river. Unlike the Kucha River, this was a dry ribbon of crystalized salt that had been washed out of the mountains to the north by rainstorms. The beacon tower was built here in the third century to keep watch over the road that led out of the mountains. It was the same road we had followed the previous day on our way into town. The tower stood fifteen meters high, and the wooden struts that once supported a viewing platform on top were still in place. A sign at the foot of the mud walls called it the Kizdorha Earth Tower. In the Uighur language, "Kizdorha" means "Don't die, daughter."

Legend had it that Kucha was once ruled by a tyrant who loved his daughter dearly. And one day a shaman told the king that his daughter would die if she had any contact with anyone during the next one hundred days. To guard against this prophecy, the king sent his daughter to live in this beacon tower and used a rope pulley to keep her supplied with food and drink. On the ninety-ninth day, the king sent his daughter an apple, her favorite fruit. But when she bit into it, a scorpion came out of it and stung her, and she lapsed into a coma. Overcome with grief, the tyrant prostrated himself at the foot of the tower and cried, "Don't die, daughter." But she never regained consciousness. And so the king learned that tragedy visits us all, even the powerful. Ever since then, the local people have called the place Don't Die Daughter Tower.

After visiting what remained of the tower, we proceeded to the Buddhist caves that once made Kucha the artistic rival of Tunhuang. The first set weren't far away. They were located across the dry bed of another river among a set of rock cliffs—there were more than forty caves. Our guide called ahead, and an attendant met us and unlocked the steel doors one at a time. I'm not sure why the authorities spent so

Don't Cry Daughter Tower

Road to Kizil Thousand Buddha Caves

much money on steel doors. There wasn't much to see: a few patches of paint and the occasional buddha with its eyes gouged out. Once again we were a century too late. Once again the German archaeologist von Le Coq had beaten us to the best frescoes and carted them off to Berlin. A frustrated Russian visitor apparently expressed similar disappointment on the bare wall of one cave. We couldn't read his comments, but they were dated November 6, 1939, just after the start of the last Great War.

We returned to our jeep and continued through the mountains to another much larger set of caves an hour to the northwest. These were the Kizil Thousand Buddha Caves, located along a series of cliffs overlooking the Kizil River. "Kizil" means "red" in the Uighur language. After parking our jeep and registering with the caretakers, we proceeded up a new metal staircase that provided access to several dozen surviving caves. Von Le Coq had been here too, but at least he didn't take everything, if only because some of the caves had been covered up by landslides. In fact, he narrowly missed being crushed to death twice during his stay here, and visitors are advised to keep an eye out for falling rocks.

While we were climbing the metal staircase that led to the surviving caves, our guide noted that until the advent of the motor car, Silk Road travelers preferred to follow rivers whenever possible, which was why the monks chose such spots for their caves: alms for the Buddha, prayers for a safe journey. Not long after the Kizil River passes the caves, it links up with the Kucha River that flows into the Tarim River that skirts the northern edge of the Taklamakan Desert before finally disappearing into the Lop Nor Desert. If travelers timed their trip when these rivers were at their peak, they could be assured of water to within a week of Tunhuang. And once past Tunhuang, there was a relatively stable water supply in the Kansu Corridor.

As we turned our attention from the river to the caves, our guide informed us that since the Chinese government had taken over the place, they had uncovered more than two hundred caves, a third of which still had frescoes of varying degrees of excellence. The artists of the Kucha area were among the best on the entire Silk Road, and their renderings were more heavily influenced by the Grecian art of Bactria and the kingdoms of Northwest India than the artistic styles of China.

The first cave we entered was filled with scaffolding, atop which a Chinese art student was lying while he sketched the frescoes that covered the ceiling. He was painting a scene in which the Buddha, in one of his previous incarnations, met a hungry tigress. This was one of the most popular tales depicted by Silk Road artists. It was the story of an Indian prince named Mahasattva who was wandering one day in the royal forest with his two princely brothers, Mahadeva and Mahaprananda. They came upon a tigress who had only recently given birth and watched her for some time. The brothers agreed that she was too weak to hunt and would soon be forced to eat her own cubs to keep from dying of starvation. Mahasattva went somewhat further in his consideration. He thought:

> For a long time I have served this body of mine, this body that is doomed to decay. How much better to leave this mortal coil of one's own accord while the bloom of youth is still upon it. It cannot last forever. Today, let me make use of it for a purpose more sublime so it might act as a boat to carry me across the sea of birth and death and I might gain the farther shore of bliss divine.

Imbued with such thoughts, Mahasattva asked his brothers to leave him alone with the tigress, and he took off his garments and lay down before her. But the tigress didn't move. She was too weak. Mahasattva was not to be denied. He got up and returned a few minutes later with a sharp piece of bamboo, and after lying down in front of the beast again, he slit his throat, and the sight of blood finally roused the tigress to action. So she ate Mahasattva, who was the Buddha in a previous lifetime, and this story has been retold ever since in words and in art to remind the faithful that charity is the greatest of all virtues and that the more you give, the more you receive.

Over the course of an hour, our guide showed us several dozen other caves, but she noted that the best frescoes were on the backside of the mountain. Unfortunately, only specialists or visitors prepared to pay beaucoup bucks were allowed to visit those particular caves, which landslides had previously hidden from foreign-devil art collectors.

Finn and I were somewhat disappointed by the limited number of frescoes open to ordinary visitors like ourselves, but we didn't feel like paying the exorbitant fees being charged to see the newly discovered ones. We turned our attention, instead, to the stream that flowed from the gorge separating the east and the west sections of the caves. We followed it for less than a kilometer to the Veil of Tears, where our guide told us a story about how the caves came to be.

It seems that another ruler of Kucha had a daughter, the beautiful Princess Chaoerhan. One day Chaoerhan chanced to meet a handsome stone carver, and the two fell in love, and the stone carver asked the king for the princess's hand in marriage. The king wasn't about to let a common stone carver marry his lovely daughter and said: "Since you're a stone carver, carve me a thousand caves. Only then will I agree to this marriage." And so the stone carver set to work. It was an impossible task, and three years later the princess found the stone carver's wasted body in that very gorge where her tears still flow between the cliffs lined with the caves her lover carved. It was a sad story. Hearing it, we lost interest in caves. We also lost interest in Kucha. We felt like we'd carved enough caves.

阿克蘇

16. Aksu

A FTER COLLECTING OUR BAGS FROM our hotel, we asked our jeep driver to take us to the Kucha bus station. Unfortunately, the next bus to Aksu wasn't due to leave for four hours. But Kucha was, after all, on the Silk Road. Instead of waiting inside the station, we walked out to the road that ran through the center of town, where there were buses from other places passing through. An hour later, we were on one of them, and we even had seats. Seats, though, didn't mean a quick trip. This one included a one-hour delay for a traffic accident, then a thirty-minute gas station stop to make sure we arrived in Aksu with a full tank.

It was early evening when we finally pulled into town. Aksu was one of the strangest towns on the Silk Road—a town in serious doubt about its identity. The authorities apparently decided Aksu was destined to become another Los Angeles and started spreading key services into the surrounding desert, hoping the town would fill in later.

Our first stop was the Friendship Hotel on the eastern outskirts. It was brand new, overpriced, and definitely meant for tour groups. Not that there was that much to see in Aksu. But being halfway between Kucha and Kashgar, Aksu was a convenient place for tours to spend the night. We retreated back to the center of town to the more modest lodgings of the old Aksu Guesthouse and ate dinner across the street at a Muslim restaurant that served the best shao-k'ao-jou this side of Heaven—shao-k'ao-jou being thin pieces of beef that have first been barbequed then

fried—and would you believe washed down with Jameson's Irish whis-key, available just down the street at the Aksu Department Store for a mere twenty bucks a bottle. We could have done a lot worse than Aksu on the Silk Road.

Other than enjoying a decent dinner and a fine bottle of whiskey, there wasn't much to do in Aksu. There was an excursion, if you had the time—which we didn't—or the money—which we didn't—or the nerve—which we also lacked. The time: three or four days. The money: $60 a day for a taxi, which included days when the taxi would have to wait. And the nerve: a hundred kilometers north of Aksu is the highest peak in the Tienshan Mountains: Mount Tomur.

Mount Tomur is over 7,400 meters, or 22,000 feet high—just a breath below Heaven. To find anything higher on the planet, you would have to visit the Himalayas. Tomur's main peak wasn't scaled for the first time until 1977, when a team of Chinese climbers finally made it to the top. Three years later, the Chinese government set up a nature reserve that encompassed the main peak and 1,000 square kilometers of the surrounding area, including several glaciers. Naturally, there aren't any roads to the top. But taxis could take people to within a two-day hike of one very big mountain and a trip they were not likely to forget. We decided to limit our Aksu experience to a night at the old guesthouse.

Aksu was once the capital of a Silk Road kingdom known as Baluka, and its residents were Indo-Europeans. But that was a long time ago. Nowadays, you would have to go to Urumchi or Chiayukuan or Lan-chou to find a more Chinese city on the Silk Road. Although represen-tatives of the Chinese government visited Aksu as early as the second century BC, they didn't extend their influence over the oasis and its sur-rounding kingdom until the first century AD. Over the centuries the Chinese maintained their presence, although it hadn't always been to their advantage. The local inhabitants periodically sent them packing or revenged earlier wrongs in other, less peaceful, ways. But the lure of trade always brought the Chinese back. Nowadays it was oil in the nearby Taklamakan Desert and produce from the irrigation projects along the Tarim River. Over the past few decades Aksu had become the biggest Chinese presence in this part of the Silk Road, with more than 150,000 Han Chinese. In fact, it's the last major Chinese population center before the various branches of the Silk Road wind their way past Kashgar into Kyrgyzstan, Afghanistan, and Pakistan.

In any case, it was not the sort of city where we wanted to linger, and we made our first order of business a ticket out of town. One option we considered was flying across the Taklamakan to the southern branch of the Silk Road, but we were told the plane only flew once or twice a week, and we picked the wrong day to be there. The Taklamakan is one of the most forbidding places on the planet after Antarctica. To put it in perspective, Hsinchiang is the biggest province in China, at 700,000 square kilometers in area, and the Taklamakan Desert occupies half of that. "Taklamakan" is Turkish for "the place where all is lost." It has definitely lived up to its reputation, swallowing whole caravans—even in modern times. One group of Western travelers who skirted the edges of the Taklamakan in the 1950s say their route was littered with the bones of those who had gone before them. More likely than not, the bones belonged to travelers who made mistakes in calculating their water supply or in navigation. On the ocean, you can miss land by as much as the distance to the nearest horizon and still make the necessary correction. In the desert, you can't afford to miss an oasis by more than the next sand dune.

Occupying an area of 335,000 square kilometers, the Taklamakan is one of the world's biggest deserts. If you look at a map of the province, you'll see a dotted line leading north from Hotien across the desert all the way to Aksu. The dotted line isn't a road. It's the Hotien River. The river, or its tributaries, originate in the Kunlun Mountains at the northern edge of the Tibetan Plateau. Some summers, melting snow fills the Hotien River with enough water to make it all the way across the Taklamakan to join several other rivers south of Aksu to form the Tarim River. In ancient times, the Hotien River's dry riverbed provided the only sure route across the Taklamakan—assuming you could find it.

The river also provided a seemingly inexhaustible supply of jade that it washed down from the Kunlun Mountains during the summer. Until

View of the Taklamakan Desert from our bus

the supply finally gave out in modern times, Hotien supplied China with much of its best jade. In the early years of Chinese civilization, it simply wasn't jade unless it came from Hotien. The Chinese called it "jade from beyond the passes," as opposed to jade from inside China. And most of the jade found in ancient Chinese graves has been traced to that Silk Road kingdom.

Hotien is the modern name of the ancient kingdom of Khotan. For many centuries Khotan was the most prosperous of all Silk Road kingdoms. And some historians have wondered about Khotan's connection with China even to the point of suggesting that the ancient residents of Khotan were somehow connected with the ancestors of the Chinese. During the decades since the current regime came to power, Chinese historians have been reluctant to pursue this connection due to possible conflicts with the reigning view that Chinese culture arose and flowered in vitro, that is, on its own. But ever since the end of the Cultural Revolution, Chinese archaeologists have begun making some rather surprising discoveries along the Silk Road, suggesting that the ideas and technology typically associated with Chinese culture reached China from as far away as Europe.

In 1984, archaeologists working just east of Hotien uncovered a series of 2,500-year-old graves that included carvings, pottery, and textiles covered with such famous heroes of Greek mythology as Athena, Hercules, and the half-man, half-horse form of Sagittarius. Further study has determined that these graves belonged to the nomadic Scythians who controlled most of Asia Minor 2,500 years ago. Unfortunately, 2,500 years only takes us halfway back to the beginnings of Chinese culture. But if the Scythians could make it that far, why not the Babylonians, refugees from the Tower of Babel?

When travelers leaving China reached the oasis of Tunhuang, they had a choice: the northern Silk Road via Hami and Turfan or the southern Silk Road via Khotan, or Hotien as the Chinese now call it. Depending on political conditions, the southern route was the route preferred by most travelers heading for India, and Khotan had close links with the cultures of the subcontinent. When the Chinese monk Hsuan-tsang passed through on his way back from India, he recorded this story about the founding of Khotan.

It seems that when King Ashoka ruled India in the third century BC, his wife died, and he remarried a much younger, more passionate woman. His new wife took a liking to his son, the crown prince, whose skin was the color of the Ganges at sunset, and whose hair was as thick and as dark as the jungle where the panther and tiger live, and whose body was as strong and smooth as the banyan tree in the palace courtyard. When the crown prince remained unmoved by his stepmother's attempts at seduction, she became furious. With the help of the crown prince's own advisors, she accused the king's son of rebellion and had his eyes gouged out and had him exiled to the deserts of Rajasthan. But such an injustice infuriated the gods, and before the year was out they were dancing on the queen's funeral pyre. When King Ashoka finally found out the truth about his son, he banished the crown prince's former advisors and their families to the land north of the Himalayas. After crossing the Tibetan Plateau, they settled in the plain where the Hotien River flowed out of the mountains. And there they founded the kingdom of Khotan, and that was the story their descendants told Hsuan-tsang.

Thus, the Scythians were followed by the Indians. In any case, whoever ruled Khotan controlled the trade in jade, and the Chinese came to know about Khotan long before there was any official contact. It turns out the people of Khotan were a sensuous lot, and the earliest mention of that distant Silk Road kingdom in Chinese records involved the dance of the swirling veils.

It seems that the beautiful Lady Ch'i became quite good at this dance when it arrived in the capital of Ch'ang-an in the baggage of jade merchants from Khotan. And when Lady Ch'i showed this dance to Emperor Kao, the founder of the Han dynasty, he became—as the dynastic records put it—most aroused. Well, one thing led to another, and before long Lady Ch'i bore the emperor a son, and she asked the emperor to make her son the new crown prince in place of the empress's son. This was a big mistake. The empress's name was Lu, and when the emperor died, Empress Lu took control of the government. The first thing she did was to get rid of Lady Ch'i's son, who got off light with a simple execution. As for Lady Ch'i, Empress Lu had her hands and feet chopped off and her eyes gouged out, then had her thrown into the palace latrine. Empress Lu was not a woman to be trifled with, and obviously she didn't have anything good to say about the dance of the swirling veils. But like it or not, that was Khotan's first mention in Chinese annals 2,200 years ago.

Due to constant climate changes, the boundaries of Khotan were never fixed, and the capital shifted from time to time due to changes in water sources. Visitors to Hotien, though, can still see the remains of at least two such sites. One is Yotkan, ten kilometers west of Hotien. And another is Melikwat, twenty-five kilometers to the south, on the way to the airport. The current consensus among historians is that Melikwat was the capital of the kingdom from the third century BC until the arrival of Islam in the tenth century AD, while Yotkan was a city of secondary importance during the same period.

For those hankering after a more authentic Silk Road experience, visitors can also organize their own expedition to other ruins, including those of Dandan-ulik, two hundred kilometers to the northeast, inside

Camels grazing in the Taklamakan

the Taklamakan—eleven days by camel, according to those who made the journey in the past. Dandan-ulik was where Aurel Stein made the first of his discoveries that began the rush to uncover the lost cities of Central Asia.

Many people have wondered why such once-flourishing cities were abandoned. Basically, the steady rise of the Tibetan Plateau cut off Central Asia from the rainfall of the Indian Ocean monsoons, which resulted in less and less snowfall at the northern edge of the Plateau as well as increasing aridity in the basin that formed to the north. Rivers that flowed as far as Dandan-ulik eventually dried up, the basin became a desert, and life became as fragile as a will-o'-the-wisp.

By the time Aurel Stein discovered the ruins in 1900, local treasure hunters had beaten him to any gold or jewels that might have remained. But careful excavation yielded more than a hundred and fifty frescoes and statues, as well as numerous coins and other items of daily use. As luck would have it, the first thing Stein found was a painting on a wooden board. It depicted a human figure with the head of a rat. And on the rat's head was a crown of jewels. And the rat was flanked by two attendants. The picture was that of the Rat King, and Stein concluded Dandan-ulik must have been part of the kingdom of Khotan.

Earlier, when Hsuan-tsang arrived at the capital of Khotan in the seventh century, he asked about a succession of small hills he had traveled through west of town. The local people told him that the hills had been formed by the burrowing of the town's sacred rats. The rats were fed and protected by the people of Khotan because they had once saved their kingdom from an invading army of Huns. It seems that while the Huns camped outside the walls of Khotan, the Rat King led his followers out of their burrows, and they ate the leather harnesses and leather armor of the Hun army. When the Huns awoke the next morning, they thought they had been victimized by ghosts, and they ran off in fright. Thus, the Rat King was worshipped in every temple in the kingdom, even in those in the middle of the Taklamakan Desert, which is where Dandan-ulik was located, two hundred kilometers north of Hotien.

All Finn and I could do was imagine such a journey. No one we talked to at our hotel knew when the once-or-twice-a-week flight to Hotien left. And when we called the next morning, no one at the airline office answered the phone. Presumably, there weren't enough people interested in flying to Hotien to warrant selling tickets. We had no choice but to continue heading west on the next bus.

喀什

17. Kashgar

A ND HEAD WEST WAS WHAT WE DID. It took all day, but eight
hours after leaving Aksu, we arrived in Kashgar, which was as
far west as we could go on the Silk Road and still be in China. Of the
200,000 people who called Kashgar home, 75 percent were Uighurs.
The figure for the surrounding area was even higher, at 92 percent. The
Chinese call Hsinchiang a "Uighur autonomous region," but any autonomy is in name only, and in the face of ethnic repression, protests and
acts of violence are common. Kashgar, especially, has been the scene of

uprisings against its Han Chinese masters. Fortunately for us, it recently had been reopened to foreigners prior to our arrival.

The earliest mention of Kashgar in historical records was by Persian writers, who noted the city's presence as a trade center maintained by a confederation of nomadic tribes. That was 2,500 years ago. Since then, the city's fortunes have waxed and waned as various nomadic groups competed for control. But even as its fortunes waned, the city's location at the confluence of two of the three main routes connecting East and West assured its eventual return to prosperity. As we arrived, it was prosperity time again, especially since the easing of border tensions between China and the former Soviet Union republics.

Despite its size, Kashgar didn't have a lot of hotel options. Of the four where foreigners were allowed to stay, we chose the Chini Bagh. It was the former residence of the British ambassador, and there was a bar in the lobby purveying cold beer to foreigners and lemonade to Pakistanis. The presence of the Pakistanis made our decision easy. The Chini Bagh was where most of them stayed while they were in Kashgar and where the chartered buses left from that traveled across the Khunjerab Pass. Unfortunately, when we checked in, we learned that while we were working our way there, monsoon rains had washed out sections of the road in Pakistan and had buried other sections beneath mountains of boulders. No one seemed to know when the road would reopen, which meant we might have to fly home via Urumchi. The euphoria we felt on our arrival vanished. After dropping our bags in our room, we walked down the street and looked for a place to eat. Along the way, we stopped at a store selling carpets, and I bought one the size of a prayer mat from the legendary city of Samarkand. The merchant said for a little extra he would tell me how to make it fly. Alas, he was joking. Kashgar was full of mysteries and disappointments. Dinner, too. The Uighur restaurant where we ate didn't serve beer, cold or otherwise. That was enough disappointment for one day.

The next morning there was still no news about the road, at least not good news, so we decided to occupy our time with the city's sights. We began with the Aidkah Mosque. Outside the hotel we flagged down a

Aidkah Mosque

Donkey transport in Kashgar

taxi. That there were taxis was a new experience. We hired the driver for the day, and a few minutes later, we were standing outside the mosque. It was located in the heart of the old town, and there were still bullet holes in the walls and a few soldiers standing in front to remind the faithful who put those holes there. The mosque was first built in 1442 on the site of an ancient cemetery. The current version was only a hundred years old, but it was the largest mosque in China. On Fridays as many as 10,000 worshippers came here to pray, many of them from distant villages there for the weekend to attend Kashgar's famous Sunday bazaar. The mosque was also the location of the province's Islamic academy, and religious leaders came here from Muslim communities all over China for special courses in Arabic and Islamic studies.

Kashgar had the unique distinction of being the gate through which both Buddhism and Islam entered China. Buddhism arrived in the first century BC, and Islam arrived eight centuries later while Muhammad was still alive. Part of the success of Islam was its message of universal brotherhood, which united the Arabs for the first time and fostered the missionary zeal that has made Islam as feared as it is loved. After

Muhammad died in 632, Islam split into two sects: the Sunnis, who recognized a series of caliphs as the rightful successors of Muhammad, and the Shiites, who followed hereditary leaders who traced their ancestry to Muhammad's daughter, Fatima. The Uighurs are Shiites, and they have been Shiites ever since the King of Kashgar accepted Islam and insisted everyone in his kingdom accept it as well.

His name was Satuk Bughra Khan. A number of bughra khans had ruled Kashgar—"bughra" being Turkish for "camel of the people." But Satuk was the first. It seems that one day when Satuk was out hunting, he saw a rabbit dart behind a bush, and when he approached the bush, the rabbit suddenly transformed itself into a man. The apparition proceeded to question Satuk about his Buddhist beliefs and convinced him that by following such beliefs he would go to Hell, whereas by following the teachings of Muhammad he would go to Heaven.

Satuk was not one to spend time considering the philosophical ramifications of such a choice, especially when the apparition explained to him that the paradise guaranteed by Muhammad included wine, women, and song. Satuk accepted Islam and not long afterwards launched a series of wars that obliterated Buddhism as an active faith on his section of the Silk Road. Satuk died in 955 and was buried forty kilometers north of Kashgar just outside the town of Artush. The original tomb was one of the Silk Road's jewels of Islamic architecture until it was destroyed by an earthquake, and our driver said the new version was far less imposing. He encouraged us to visit something else instead.

Satuk, it turns out, wasn't the only ruler of Kashgar to gain fame throughout the Islamic world. After visiting the city's main mosque, we drove three kilometers east of town to the family tomb of Abakh Khoja. For Muslims, this is the holiest place in all of Hsinchiang. For nonbelievers it is also worthy of a visit, if only for the architecture. Passing through the blue-and-white-tiled gate, we were suddenly back in the Ming dynasty locked in a battle between the White Mountain and Black Mountain sects of Islam.

The tomb is where Abakh Khoja was buried in 1694, but it also contains the remains of other members of the same lineage, including the

Tomb of Abakh Khoja

remains of Abakh's father, Yussup Khoja. Four hundred years ago, the people of the palm-fringed oasis of Kashgar were ruled by a hereditary line of holy men known as khojas. And it came to pass that one such khoja had thirteen sons. But before he named his successor, he died. This oversight left the religious and political leadership of Kashgar open to dispute, and the sons chose sides—as if they were contesting a game of cricket. But the game soon got out of hand, and the brothers started killing each other, and thus began the two sects of Islam that ever since have contended for the souls of the faithful in Hsinchiang.

In the ensuing struggle, the leadership of Kashgar passed to one of the sons who had recently returned from a pilgrimage to the holy sites of Islam. The son's name was Yussup. He was a vocal proponent of purity of practice, and the sect of which he became the head was soon dubbed the white cap sect, as opposed to the black cap sect of his opponents. Over time, these two also became known as the White Mountain and Black Mountain sects, and you can still tell to which one a person belongs by simply looking at their cap. Unfortunately for Yussup Khoja, a member of the black cap sect put a white cap on one day and managed to get close enough to stick a knife into Yussup's heart. And here he lay, inside the loveliest of mausoleums at the east edge of town.

After his death, Yussup was succeeded by his eldest son Abakh, and Abakh became Kashgar's most famous khoja. During the course of his long career, he spent several decades as a wandering prophet and several more as king of this kingdom that included the western half of Hsinchiang. At one time his followers numbered as many as 300,000, and the inhabitants of towns under his sway who didn't become members of the White Mountain sect were put to death. Like his father before him, he was killed by a Black Mountain assassin, and his remains were also placed inside the mausoleum he built for his father.

Among Chinese Muslims who trace their ancestry to his White Mountain sect, Abakh Khoja is revered almost as much as Muhammad, and they consider a pilgrimage to the mausoleum that contains his and his father's remains second only in importance to a visit to Mecca. The mausoleum is also said to hold the remains of other relatives, including those of Abakh Khoja's granddaughter, Iparhan.

In Uighur, "Iparhan" means "Perfumed Lady," for when Iparhan was born her skin had a fragrance like sweet dates. When she was a young girl she was sent to Beijing, where she attended the emperor for twenty-five years until she died. Her body was carried back to Kashgar in a cortege that took three years to arrive. Some historians say she was, in fact, buried near Beijing and that only her clothes were brought back to Kashgar. Such was her fame, though, people in Kashgar sometimes forget that Abakh Khoja is buried here at all and call this "The Tomb of the Perfumed Lady."

After visiting her tomb and that of her grandfather and great-grandfather, we considered visiting yet another tomb, namely, the tomb of Muhammad al-Kashgari. Despite his name, which translates as Muhammad of Kashgar, al-Kashgari was born in the town of Upar, forty-five kilometers west of Kashgar, and he didn't come to Kashgar until his father inherited the kingdom in the early part of the eleventh century. Unfortunately, there were those who were jealous of his father, and they poisoned his father and his entire court, all except al-Kashgari, who managed to escape with his life.

Tomb of Hachi Hachip

For more than ten years, al-Kashgari wandered among the Turk-ish-speaking nomads and farming communities northwest of Kashgar, and he began recording detailed information about their histories and customs as well as their languages. Eventually, he reached the city of Bukhara, which was one of the leading centers of learning in the Islamic world. He spent three years there recording his observations and compiled the first and only dictionary of the ancient Turkish language, for which scholars of Central Asian languages are extremely grateful. After being lost for many centuries, al-Kashgari's magnum opus was unearthed in Turkey during the early twentieth century, and it is now one of the prize possessions of the national museum in Istanbul. As for al-Kashgari's bones, they are the prize possession of his hometown west of Kashgar. But once again, our driver convinced us to visit a different tomb, one closer to Kashgar.

The tomb toward which he drove us belonged to Yussup Hachi Hachip. Hachi Hachip came to Kashgar as a young boy in the eleventh century, and he spent most of his remaining years here. In the course of his studies, he became especially fond of poetry, and later in life, when he was in his fifties, he composed a long poem entitled "Pleasure and Wisdom," in which he used the voices of the morning sun, the full moon, reason, and awareness to extol pleasure and wisdom as the necessary counterparts of a good life. His poem is 13,000 lines long, and one wonders how the local potentate managed to sit still to hear it all. But sit still he did, and when Hachi Hachip finished, the ruler was so impressed he elevated Hachi Hachip to royal status. His poem became famous throughout the Islamic world. It was written in the early script used by the Uighurs, and one such edition dating back to the year 1439 still survives in the state museum in Vienna.

Our driver told us Hachi Hachip's mausoleum was destroyed during the Cultural Revolution, but it had been rebuilt. Once again, we were there in a matter of minutes. Clearly our driver was intent on avoiding the roads outside Kashgar, and we assumed he was right in doing so. He was also right about the mausoleum. It was in fine shape, complete with a garden of roses in full bloom. Inside on one of the mausoleum walls was carved a Chinese translation of Hachi Hachip's entire poem in Uighur and in Chinese. After reading a few stanzas, it was clear that Omar Khayyam had read it too—though not the Chinese version. Omar died in 1123, several decades after Hachi Hachip, and he expressed much the same sentiments as the great poet of Kashgar:

> *Make the most of what you yet may spend*
> *before you too into the dust descend*
> *dust into dust*
> *and under dust to lie*
> *sans wine, sans song, sans singer, sans end.*

I'm not sure how all this talk of pleasure went down with the stricter, lemonade-drinking members of the Islamic world, but Kashgar's Uighurs obviously held him in the highest esteem. Hachi Hachip's tile-covered mausoleum and well-tended rose garden were an oasis unto themselves. Once again, we turned to our driver and suggested an excursion outside of town. We had heard that there was a Buddhist stupa at a place called Hanoi. Before Islam's sword of purity began ridding the Silk Road of infidels in the ninth century, most of the people who lived along the Silk Road followed the path of the Buddha. And at the oasis of Hanoi they left behind a singular monument to their faith. In fact, it was the only evidence that Buddhism was once alive and well in the Kashgar area. It was curious, though, that the stupa was still standing. It represented the stupa's earliest form: smooth sides and a round top. Our driver said it looked like a penis, which made us wonder why the various Islamic purges experienced in the Kashgar region had left it alone. But any thought of going there was soon quashed. Our driver said the road there was too torn up for his taxi.

That pretty much exhausted our list of places to see in the Kashgar area, all except one. And this time our driver was only too happy to take us there. A few minutes later, we arrived at Kashgar's Sunday bazaar. It was the afternoon, but it was still going strong. This is the most famous weekly market in China, and it's probably the oldest, dating back to the second century BC. If you look at a map, you'll notice that Kashgar is halfway between China and the Mediterranean. It's 3,500 kilometers either way. In ancient times, few merchants carried their goods the entire length of the Silk Road. Most only went as far as their baksheesh ensured them of safe passage. They then sold or traded their goods and headed back home. Being halfway between the source of silk and its biggest market, Kashgar was the end of the line for many merchants, and despite all the havoc wrought by the twentieth century, its bazaar has continued unchanged.

Kashgar also has other bazaars in other parts of town on other days. But the Sunday bazaar at the east edge of town is the grandmother of them all. It consists of six areas, each with twenty sections, and each offering its own particular line of merchandise. Some sections are devoted entirely to hats, others to boots or knives or copper pots or bales of cotton or bolts of silk. Others specialize in animal feed or the animals themselves. A fine horse bred by a Tajik nomad in the grasslands of the nearby Pamirs, we learned, cost a mere 1,000RMB, or $200.

According to local officials, an average Sunday attracts anywhere from 50,000 to 100,000 people. As with any bazaar, prices aren't carved in stone, and not only are they subject to negotiation, they tend to drop as the day wears on. We spent nearly two hours touring the stalls and ended up buying a few gifts to take home, the most notable of which were Yengisar knives from the nearby city of Yingchisha and multicolored silk that the Uighurs called "moonlight." The knives were set with colored glass, and their steel blades shimmered in the afternoon sun. And the silk was irresistible, as silk so often is. We reasoned that neither the knives nor the silk would take up much room in our bags—not that we needed reasons. Speaking of our bags, that reminded us, it was time to find out if there was any news about our next destination and how we were going to get there.

And so we returned to the lobby of the Chini Bagh to sift through rumors, which was probably the oldest and most popular Kashgar pastime. The Chini Bagh was where the British Consulate used to be, and the former Russian Consulate was just down the street masquerading as the West Gate Hotel. A hundred years earlier, when Russia, Britain, and China vied for control of Central Asia, these two consulates, along with the local Chinese yamen, housed the principal adversaries in what became known as the Great Game. During the heady days of imperialist expansion, the empires of China, Russia, and Britain all met in Kashgar. For its part, China had preceded its rivals here by two hundred years. But Moscow was just as close as Beijing, and Delhi was a lot closer than either.

By the time we arrived, the Great Game was over, and Kashgar was once again a city of merchants, especially Pakistani merchants. The landslides that closed the only road home had been a disaster for them. Many had started reselling what they had bought to pay for another meal or another night at the Chini Bagh. Although there was no news, good or bad, a Pakistani sitting at the table next to us later that night at dinner said his government was planning to charter several 747s to take him and his countrymen home. But he didn't know when that might happen. Another Pakistani cautioned patience, the road would reopen in a few more days. But a Pakistani tour operator said it was still too

Camels grazing along the Ghez River

dangerous, an American girl who tried to cross one of the landslides had been killed by a boulder the previous day, and the Chinese authorities were telling everyone the road wouldn't reopen for months, if at all.

While the Pakistanis continued trading rumors—and in truth they didn't have anything better to do—we finished our dinner and went back to our room, and finally decided we couldn't wait. If we couldn't continue on to Islamabad, we would have to go back the way we came and resolved to settle the issue one way or the other the following day. And that was what we did. But we took our time. We slept late. We skipped breakfast and began the day with a couple of beers in the hotel lobby. We were hoping there would be some news. But there wasn't. So we walked down the street to buy plane tickets back to Sian via Urumchi. But when we reached the local airline office, the front door was locked. It was only eleven o'clock, but a sign said CLOSED FOR LUNCH. We decided to wait and joined another foreigner sitting in the shade. He was from Australia. Like us, he was waiting to buy a ticket to Urumchi to spare himself the agony of the three-day bus ride. But unlike us, he hadn't come from Urumchi. He said he had just arrived from Islamabad.

What? Islamabad? Wasn't the road closed? Well, yes and no. He said there were landslides all right, but there were trucks and vans waiting to carry people from one slide to the next. That was all we needed to hear, and back we went to the Chini Bagh to spread the news. Apparently we weren't the only ones to meet a recent arrival from south of the border. We no sooner returned to the hotel than the front desk announced the sale of bus tickets. A convoy was leaving the next morning. All the Pakistanis sitting in the lobby rushed to the counter. As luck would have it, we just happened to be standing there and managed to come up with the first two tickets. They weren't cheap at 150RMB, or thirty bucks, apiece, but they were tickets on a bus to Islamabad.

Sure enough, early the next morning two hundred Pakistanis began loading what was left of their merchandise onto the roofs of the five buses that made up our caravan. It took three hours to load it all, and we didn't leave until midday. But we left. As we followed the old city

Prayer break along the Ghez River

wall west out of town, no one said a word. No one believed it was actually happening. We expected to turn back at any moment. But we kept going.

Once we were beyond the city wall, it wasn't long before we entered a landscape barren of everything but rocks, and we began following the Ghez River upstream into a long, narrow valley of wine-red sandstone cliffs that rose straight out of the river. As the road wound higher and higher onto the Pamir Plateau, my altimeter went from 1,300 meters to 3,200. After struggling over our first pass, the driver stopped, and all the Pakistanis got out, washed their feet in the icy stream at the side of the road, unrolled their prayer rugs, and joined us in praying for our bus.

往塔什庫尔干

18. The Road to Tashkorgan

AFTER OUR BRIEF NOD IN THE direction of Mecca, we continued on across a series of half-dry rivers and entered a landscape
picked clean of everything but rocks. It was time to say good-bye to the
Uighurs, who had taken care of us in all the Silk Road towns in which
we had we stayed. We were going to miss them, and especially their
shady oases, concerning which, of course, there is a story.

A long time ago, back when Central Asia was still covered with trees
instead of grass and sand, a mound of earth appeared one day between

two trees, and a shaft of light shone down from the sky and onto the mound, and the mound grew bigger and bigger, and the local people noticed this and thought it most strange. And they thought it most strange, indeed, when the mound split apart, and five tents appeared, and inside each tent was a baby. Most strange, indeed. The village elders concluded that the babies had been sent to them by the gods, and they took them back to their village and raised them as their own, until one day the children asked who their parents were, and the villagers took them back to the twin trees. And the trees told the children how glad they were to see them again, and the children promised to return often. And they have kept their promise. It turns out the children were the ancestors of the Uighurs. And Uighurs still pay their respects to trees. But not just to any trees, only to mother-elm trees and father-poplar trees. As we traveled through Hsinchiang, we often saw colored strips of cloth tied around an elm or poplar, which was a sign some lost member of the tree people had been asking their ancestors for guidance. But not on the road from Kashgar to Pakistan. As far as the eye could see, we saw nothing but rocks.

An hour or so after our prayer break, our driver stopped again along the edge of a lake, this time for a pee break. The Pakistanis were all dressed in their knee-length kameez shirts and squatted to pee, while Finn and I stood outside the bus and faced downwind. We all gazed in admiration at what must have been one of the most stunning scenes in China: the snowy peaks of 7,700-meter Mount Kongur and 7,500-meter Muztagh-ata shimmering in the breathless waters of Lake Karakul. During the summer, the surrounding grasslands are dotted with the yurts and herds of the Kirghiz nomads who live in this part of China. But we were here in fall, and they had moved to other, lower pastures.

"Muztagh-ata" is Uighur for "father of ice-covered mountains." Not only were the mountain's diamond-like peaks jaw-droppingly majestic, Karakul was one of the most beautiful lakes Finn and I had ever seen. Its blue surface was so dark, it was almost black. With an average depth of thirty meters, it is a very peculiar lake. It doesn't have a surface outlet—no stream drawing its water down into the valley up which we had

Lake Karakul with Mount Kongur and Muztagh-ata in the distance

been traveling. Its water flows out, instead, through underground channels beneath the nearby mountains and into springs along the southern branch of the Silk Road. It is also a sacred lake, and no one but fools swim in it. The water is ice-cold, and according to local Kirghiz herders there is a huge fish living in the lake, and every day around noon it rises to the surface, rolls over, and descends again into the blue-black depths.

It was late afternoon, and there was no sign of a fish. It was also late fall, and the only Kirghiz in sight were the few who took care of the small tourist hostel near the place where we stopped. But there weren't any tourists. Finn and I waved at the caretakers, and they waved back. We guessed they hadn't seen any buses for months, ever since the landslides toward which we were heading blocked the road. We climbed back on board and our caravan continued on.

At the time of our trip, there were 150,000 Kirghiz living in China, and most of them were living in the foothills and high plateaus of the Pamirs along China's borders with Afghanistan, Tajikistan, and, of course, Kyrgyzstan—which was the ancient Kirghiz homeland and home to a million more pony-riding, sheep-herding, tale-telling nomads. One of the tales the Kirghiz tell is about how there came to be any Kirghiz left in this part of China, or in Kyrgyzstan for that matter. It seems that a long time ago, when the entire Kirghiz tribe could fit inside a dozen yurts, another tribe swept down one day and massacred everyone except one boy and one girl who happened to be gathering medicinal plants in the nearby mountains.

When the children returned and saw what had happened, they were overcome with grief, and would have cried themselves to death. But as luck would have it, a kind old mother deer came along and carried them into the woods. The deer nursed them with her milk and led them through the forest to collect nuts and berries. And the children eventually grew up, and they had children, and their children had children. And that is why there are still Kirghiz on the shores of Lake Karakul and the slopes of Muztagh-ata.

Another story the Kirghiz like to tell on long winter nights is about how the sun and moon came to be. It seems that when the god of the universe made the world, among the many creatures he made was the fire spirit, and the fire spirit loved to burn, and before long it was burning everything and everyone in sight, and all the creatures cried for help, and when the god of the universe saw what was happening, it was very upset and told the fire spirit to stop. But the fire spirit didn't pay any attention. It kept burning everything it could get its flames on.

This was too much for the god of the universe. It transformed itself into a huge blue ox with horns twenty kilometers long, and it snorted and charged the fire spirit. And the two locked horns, and they fought until finally the fire spirit cried out for mercy and asked the sky spirit for a place to hide. The sky spirit, it turned out, was a kindhearted spirit, and it opened up the blue vault of Heaven, and the fire spirit flew up to the sky, where it was out of the reach of the horns of the god of the universe. And from its perch in the sky, the fire spirit once more started burning everything on Earth, and all the creatures cried out. The god of the universe then sent the ice spirit into the sky, and it flew up and sent cool breezes and rainfall down onto the Earth, and all the creatures were saved, including the ancestors of the Kirghiz who still tell this story on long winter nights about how the sun and moon came to be and how important all that snow outside their tents was.

Speaking of the cold, as the sun slipped behind the Pamir Plateau, the temperature inside the bus dropped through the floor. Since our overnight stop was still two hours away, I reached into my pack and pulled out my first bottle of Chinese brandy. In addition to sharing the bus with several dozen Pakistani merchants, there were also several foreigners, one of whom was sitting right behind us. His name was John, and he was from Australia. And not long after passing him our bottle, John warmed us up with this:

> *The Karakoram is a bloody long road*
> *there're camels and buses to carry your load*
> *there're yaks with fur*
> *and that comes in handy*
> *but not as much as a bottle of brandy*

This was followed by a few more swigs and a few more ditties. Finally, John collapsed in his seat. The brandy at that altitude was too much of a shock. We were rolling along at 3,600 meters, and we were still more than an hour away from our overnight stop at Tashkorgan. In addition to the area being home to Kirghiz nomads, it is also home to Tajiks. There aren't as many Tajiks in China as there are Kirghiz: only about 35,000, as opposed to 150,000. But the Tajiks have just as many stories to tell. And this is their territory, too, in the highest part of the Pamirs.

In the case of the Kirghiz, they migrated here from the Yenisei River near the present Russian city of Novosibirsk far to the north. But the Tajiks' ancient homeland was to the west. Scholars have traced their ancestry to the highlands of eastern Iran, or the edge of the ancient Persian Empire. The Tajiks started settling the Pamirs as early as 3,000 years ago, and when they arrived they brought with them the flute, which they introduced to the Chinese in the second century BC.

On the road to Tashkorgan

According to the Tajiks, it was a young Tajik named Wa-fa who made the first flute. The story they tell goes like this: there was once a family of hunters—a father, his son, and their young slave named Wa-fa. They lived a very hard life. No matter how much game they killed, it was never enough for their chief, who took it all for himself. When the father and son complained, the chief had them put to death. The chief was so greedy, he even demanded the family's only remaining possession: an old eagle the family used for catching small game.

When Wa-fa heard that the chief was coming for the eagle, he took the bird and ran off into the mountains. As soon as the chief found out, he set off with his henchmen, and they tracked Wa-fa into the mountains. Wa-fa climbed higher and higher, but it was no use. The chief and his henchmen were right behind him. Finally, when Wa-fa reached the summit, he decided to jump rather than give up the family's eagle.

The eagle had served the family for many years, and it was a kind old bird. Just as Wa-fa was getting ready to jump, the eagle bit off one of its own wings and gave it to Wa-fa. And the eagle showed Wa-fa how to make a flute out of the bone. And just as the chief and his henchmen reached him, Wa-fa blew on the flute, and a flock of eagles appeared and started attacking Wa-fa's pursuers. The chief cried out for mercy, and Wa-fa said he would spare his life if he would set free all the slaves in the village and give them sheep and cattle. The chief had no choice. And that is how the flute came to be.

Another tale the Tajiks like to tell is how we all got here. It happened a long time ago, before anyone was born, when all there was was a world. It appeared one day while An-la, the creator of the universe, was sitting in the middle of the galaxy. An-la was just sitting there, and this light was shining all around him. Or maybe An-la was a she, or maybe An-la was the pupil in the eye of an ant. In any case, suddenly an egg appeared in the light, and An-la picked up the egg and split it in two: into Heaven and Earth. Then An-la decided he would like to have some people living on Earth. So An-la called some angels and asked them to make some people. And the angels said, "In whose likeness, oh mighty one, should we make these 'people,' as you call them."

An-la answered, "Go to the lake of paradise and look into the water, and make my people in the image you see there." The angels did as they were told, and when they looked into the water, they saw their own reflections. But they had never seen reflections before, and they thought it was just another wonder worked by the creator. And so the angels made figures in their own image. But instead of making them out of light, they made them out of dirt and blew into them the spirit of Heaven and set them to walk about on the Earth, and they have been walking about ever since. And that is how we all got here. But there is still more to this story.

Once the angels made people and set them to wander around paradise, like all paradises, this was one where no one had to do any work and where everyone was happy. But people being people, they thought that maybe there was something better. And one day when they were out walking, they saw a field of wheat, and they wondered what would happen if they ate some of it, and so they ate some wheat. It tasted okay, but then something strange happened. They all got this great urge to move their bowels. They had never been hungry before, so they had never eaten anything before. And after they moved their bowels, this terrible stink started to spread over paradise. No one had ever smelled anything quite so bad before, including An-la, the creator. When An-la smelled it, he was so angry, he ordered people to leave paradise and never return. And so people wandered across the Earth. But when they did, they didn't have anything to eat, so they asked An-la for food. And An-la gave them some of the wheat they had already eaten. When they asked An-la how to plant the wheat, An-la showed them and also gave them some oxen. But the oxen asked An-la what they were supposed to eat. An-la pointed at a pile of wheat and a pile of chaff, and asked them to choose. Naturally, there was more chaff than wheat, and the oxen, being oxen, chose the chaff. And that is the way it has been ever since. People eat the wheat, and oxen eat the chaff, and together they do nothing but stink up the world. And just as Finn and I emptied our first bottle of brandy, our bus convoy pulled into Tashkorgan: the ancient capital of the storytelling Tajiks.

When the Greek geographer, Ptolemy, described the limits of the known world in the second century AD, he called Tashkorgan the westernmost town of the Land of Silk, which was the name for China in those days. This was, in fact, the main route of the silk trade then: from Kashgar over the Karakorum Range and into the Buddhist kingdoms of Northwest India. In those days, the inhabitants of Tashkorgan were called Sarikolis, and the landscape we had been crossing since leaving the Ghez River is still called the Sarikol Valley. The Sarikolis were the ancestors of the Tajiks. Unlike the Kirghiz and other nomads in the area, they depended mostly on agriculture and trade to support themselves. Except during the summer, they lived in wooden or stone houses, instead of in yurts made of felt. And Tashkorgan was the capital of their ancient mountain kingdom.

Although it was too dark to see anything when we arrived, the ruins of their capital were on a hillside just to the south. No one knew exactly when the capital was built, but it was sometime after the King of Persia had a dream about a Chinese princess. She must have been very beautiful, because when he awoke, the king sent emissaries to ask the emperor of China for her hand in marriage. That was during one of those periods when the Chinese were trying to expand their influence into Hsinchiang, and so the Chinese emperor agreed to the request and sent a princess along with a retinue of attendants. But when they reached the Sarikol Valley, it was winter, and the passes were closed, so the princess had to wait for spring. And while she was waiting, she fell in love.

When the Chinese monk Hsuan-tsang passed through Tashkorgan in the seventh century with his ponies loaded down with Buddhist scriptures, he stopped long enough to record this story before proceeding back to China. Rather than wait out the winter in the valley, the officials in charge of guarding the princess chose a nearby mountain to which access was restricted, and they built a fort there. But the officials hadn't reckoned with the ways of the mountain spirits, who had never seen such a beautiful woman before.

Sure enough, when the first blush of spring graced the apricot trees at the foot of the mountain, the officials discovered to their horror that the princess was pregnant. "What!" they shouted. "How could this have happened? We've been guarding her night and day. How could anyone have snuck inside?" They proceeded to look for a secret passage, and they threatened to execute all the princess's attendants unless they revealed who the father was. Finally, one of the maids unraveled the mystery: "Every day at noon," she said, "a handsome young man comes down from the sun and enters the princess's room and flies off again on the billowing red clouds of sunset. I've heard the princess sigh at his departure and know the two are in love."

Well, the officials sent by the emperor to convey the princess safely to Persia trembled in fear. If they continued on their journey, they knew they would be executed when the King of Persia discovered what had happened. And if they returned to China, a similar fate awaited them at the hands of the Chinese emperor. They had no choice. They decided to stay where they were. They declared the princess queen of a kingdom they called Chiehpanto. She made Tashkorgan her capital, and when her son—whose father was, in fact, the sun god—grew up, he became the king of Chiehpanto and the ancestor of the people known ever since as Tajiks. And that was the story told to Hsuan-tsang by the king of Chiehpanto when the Chinese monk passed through Tashkorgan in the seventh century.

The princess's original citadel, the place where she became pregnant, was eighty kilometers from Tashkorgan on a mountain overlooking the very road we were following. We weren't planning to visit it, but we didn't have to. Aurel Stein visited and photographed the place a hundred years earlier and demonstrated to the outside world why that site was chosen. From the citadel's sheer walls, the princess and her successors were able to keep track of travelers passing between China and what are now Pakistan and Afghanistan. At an elevation of more than 4,000 meters, it was the highest fortification in China, and one wonders how its inhabitants managed to build such a citadel, much less live in it.

As time went on, the princess's descendants decided in favor of more hospitable lodgings, and they moved their capital to the present site of Tashkorgan. "Tashkorgan" is Uighur for "stone city," and the city's original walls are still here, on a hillside at the edge of town. At least that was what we were told. We arrived at night. And all we could think of was food and sleep.

And we didn't arrive alone. We arrived along with two hundred Pakistanis in the first bus convoy to leave Kashgar for Pakistan in forty days. After ten hours on the road, all we could think of was a meal and a bed. As we checked into the bus station hotel, the girl at the desk told us the road ahead was still blocked by landslides. The slides, she said, were on the Pakistan side, and we were still a hundred kilometers short of the border. The girl added that nothing bigger than a bicycle had made it through for the past forty days and that we would have to walk sixty kilometers to get through all the slides. She laughed at the idea of our convoy making it.

We sighed at the thought of the road ahead. The road we were traveling was the Karakorum Highway, named for the mountain range it cut through on the Pakistan side. Trade routes had passed through these mountains since Neolithic times, but this was the first road ever built. Work on it began in the 1960s when China and Pakistan decided to patch up their differences to counter improving ties between India and Russia. And so, in the early 1960s, when the Pakistanis held out an olive branch, the Chinese grabbed it and ceded 2,000 square kilometers of disputed territory to Pakistan and agreed to cooperate on a cross-border highway.

The highway took 30,000 Pakistanis and Chinese laborers twenty years to build and cost more than a thousand lives. It was first opened to official traffic and cross-border trade in 1982 and to tourism in 1986. Since then, it had been closed periodically by landslides, but never for more than a few days—at least not until we showed up in the fall of 1992. But we had other concerns than the road ahead. We were famished.

Thankfully, someone from the Chini Bagh had called ahead, and the hotel restaurant was still open. I have no memory of what we ate. But while we were washing down whatever it was with beer, the electricity suddenly went off. Before we could do anything more than stare helplessly into the dark, the hotel staff reappeared just as suddenly bearing candles and started handing them out. The town, they said, turned off the electricity every night at midnight. Fortunately, we were done with dinner, and we managed to find our way to our rooms. By the time Finn and I got into bed, it was nearly one, and we were both tired. But there was one last Tajik tale to tell—a bedtime story, if you will. It was about the most famous Tajik hero, Lussu Tamu.

It seems that a Tajik warrior by the name of Samu once had a son, and when the son was born he was covered with white hair. Samu took this as an evil omen and abandoned the child in the wilds. But it so happened that the place where he abandoned the child was also where a phoenix lived. And the phoenix found the child and cared for it. Then one night the child appeared to Samu in a dream. When Samu awoke the next morning, he went looking for the child, and he found it and brought it back home. And his son grew up into a handsome young man and eventually married a girl from the land of darkness, and they had a son. And their son was so strong, he killed a lion with a wooden club, and everyone called him Lussu Tamu, the lion-killer. And he performed

The Karakorums

many miraculous deeds and defeated the forces of darkness. Tajiks say the rainbow was his weapon, and his grave is on a small hill between Tashkorgan and Muztagh-ata. Apparently our bus passed it in the darkness on our way here. It was a good thing this last story was so short. Trying to breathe the air at 4,000 meters, much less tell a story, left me exhausted. And that was all I remember.

紅其拉甫山口

19. The Khunjerab Pass

THE NEXT MORNING, FINN AND I rose with the sun ready to face another day of Silk Road uncertainty. But when we went outside, all the buses in our convoy were gone. What the hell? We rushed back inside to find out why they had left without us. Our distress was short-lived. The woman at the front desk said they had gone to fill up with gas and would be back in an hour, which they were. Finally, just after ten o'clock, we resumed our journey to Pakistan along with two hundred citizens of that Islamic republic.

From Tashkorgan, the road continued up a wide valley whose only signs of life were the occasional herds of horses or yaks or camels. At one point, we passed the Kirghiz settlement of Dabdar, where the Mintaka River enters the valley we were following from the west. Before the road was built, the old trade route to Pakistan followed the Mintaka another twenty kilometers or so then veered up and across the Mintaka Pass. "Mintaka" means "A Thousand Mountain Goats," and at 5,000 meters, the pass demands the stamina of a mountain goat. Fortunately, our destination was the less demanding Khunjerab Pass to the south, not far beyond the Chinese border post of Pirali. Pirali is where travelers must clear immigration and customs and where we arrived two hours after leaving Tashkorgan.

No vehicles had been through the pass in over a month, and no one was expecting us. After we arrived, it took another two hours to round up the proper officials with the requisite keys and the appropriate chops, which seemed especially mysterious since there were only four small buildings. Apparently, everyone was sleeping. And after they woke up, they had to have lunch. And only after they had eaten did the Chinese border officials begin considering our case.

First of all, it turned out that twenty of our two hundred fellow passengers had overstayed their visas. They were Pakistanis, and they had been stuck in Kashgar for more than forty days, ever since landslides closed the Khunjerab Pass separating China and Pakistan. The border officials were also concerned that since none of us had multiple-entry visas, if they let us through and we were unable to continue on, we would be stuck in Pirali when we tried to return without visas. Negotiations went on for two hours, while we all waited outside in the wind. We hadn't eaten breakfast, and now we were missing lunch. Dinner, of course, was nowhere in sight. A few snowflakes drifted out of the sky, and one last Tajik story came drifting down with them.

It seems that back when the world was new, whenever people were hungry, the creator sprinkled a fine flour called "manna" over the Earth, and people used the flour to make bread and noodles, and no one was ever hungry, until one day an old lady used the flour to wipe her ass.

When the creator saw this, he became so angry, he turned the flour into snow, and people have been hungry ever since, and cold too. And just as we were cursing that old lady, the Pakistani elders who had been conducting negotiations with the Chinese came outside waving our passports. They were going to let us through. The Chinese border officials had finally decided to wash their hands of us and let us all cross the border—with the understanding that unless someone had a multiple-entry visa no one would be allowed back should the Khunjerab Pass prove impassable.

As one of the border guards lifted the barrier, someone in our bus tossed a string of firecrackers out a window to scare off any ghosts we might have picked up along the way. Everyone cheered and yelled and thanked Allah, as we began our final push toward the highest pass in the world through which mankind had managed to build a road. The Khunjerab Pass is over 4,600 meters, or 15,000 feet above sea level. It is in what botanists call the Frigid Zone, and there was nothing outside our bus window but snow. During the summer, the snow melts just long enough for wild flowers to bloom, then it's back to winter. "Khunjerab" is Tajik for "Blood Valley." The name came from the blood of the packhorses through whose muzzles their owners drove iron nails to relieve the pressure from the altitude. Early Western travelers noted the blood-stained rocks that lined the way to the pass. But all we saw was snow.

From Pirali, it took us an hour to wind our way up the last, broad slopes of the Pamirs. The sign at the pass said 4,700 meters. My own altimeter put it at a shade over 4,600. The sign also said WELCOME TO PAKISTAN. As we drove by it, two hundred Pakistanis and a dozen foreigners cheered. Just below the pass, we stopped at a military checkpoint consisting of two lonesome cement huts in the middle of a snowfield. A Pakistani soldier came out. He was wearing a beret and a commando sweater and boots. He actually looked like a soldier. His uniform fit, unlike the one-size-fit-all outfits worn by his Chinese counterparts at Pirali. After a cursory examination of our passports and visas, the guard smiled, lifted the barrier and waved us through. And he kept waving until we disappeared into the dark gorge cut by the Khunjerab River

Road over the Khunjerab Pass

through the Karakorums. When Aurel Stein came through the Khunjerab Pass a hundred years earlier, he called the pass an excursion for ladies. Up until then we might have agreed with him, but it didn't take long for us to realize that he must have been talking about the Chinese side of the pass.

The broad rolling slopes of the Pamirs end at the border, and the dark, rocky cliffs of the Karakorums begin. Instead of looking for the occasional yak, we now kept our eyes peeled for big-horned Marco Polo sheep. The Karakorums are their last refuge. Meanwhile, we began a series of switchbacks that took us from 4,600 meters to less than 3,000 meters in a matter of minutes. The snow gave way to rocks, and the sunlight gave way to darkness, as we found ourselves following the Khunjerab River into a gorge that led through the Karakorums.

In Turkish, "kara" means "black" and "korum" means "loose rock." The road was, indeed, an obstacle course of boulders. But we were finally in Pakistan, and everyone was smiling. Then, just as we rounded a bend in the road, there was a crash, and the whole bus shuddered. A large boulder just missed one of the windows and hit the side of our vehicle. Instead of stopping to inspect the damage, the driver stepped on the gas, and we didn't look back. We didn't have time to look back. Around the next bend, the road was blocked by dozens of boulders, some of them bigger than our bus. Suddenly, we realized why no vehicle had made it through the pass in more than a month.

We all piled out: half a dozen Westerners, half a dozen Chinese, and two hundred Pakistanis. As we walked around and inspected the situation, it didn't look good. And no amount of walking around made it look any better. Still, we had to do something, so we began filling in holes in the road with the smaller rocks and rolling boulders into the gorge. Some of the boulders took two or three men to move, others took a dozen. But there was one boulder that even two hundred Pakistanis couldn't budge.

While we were all standing there wondering what to do next, the Chinese official in charge of the convoy told everyone to get back into the buses. He was turning the convoy around and taking us back to China. We could wait, he said, in Tashkorgan until the road could be cleared or new entry visas could be arranged.

While the Pakistanis were feigning ignorance of Chinese, and the Chinese official was trying to get the Westerners to translate, Finn and I walked over to the big boulder that blocked the road. We picked up two good-sized rocks and banged them against the side of the boulder. A chunk fell off the boulder. We hit it again, and another chunk fell off. After a few more hits, two Pakistanis came over and joined us, then two more, and two more. Pretty soon there were about fifty of us banging away at a boulder the size of a house. But the house was getting smaller. And with each disappearing chunk another cheer rose from the onlookers. Then, as the echo of the cheers died away, everyone suddenly stopped. Rocks began falling on the other side of the gorge. We all looked up at our side. There wasn't much sunlight left, and we wouldn't have seen anything until it hit us anyway. We went back to work. Finally, one huge chunk fell off the boulder, and everyone gathered around to measure the distance between the boulder and the edge

Fellow passengers clearing boulders off the road

of the cliff that formed the other edge of the road. There was just enough room for a bus, with about a foot to spare.

Unfortunately, four of the five bus drivers were Chinese, and none of them were willing to risk it. But the lone Pakistani driver agreed to try. We all held our breaths. He scraped off some paint, but he made it. Once again two hundred cheers shook a few more rocks loose from the cliffs. The other buses followed quickly, while they could, and we all returned to our seats and continued into one of the longest nights of our lives.

As we rumbled on, stopping periodically to roll away boulders, the sun went down. As it did, the first bus turned on its headlights, while the other drivers followed behind holding flashlights out their windows. I know it sounds ridiculous, but the drivers thought they would drain their batteries if they turned on their headlights. Still, it didn't matter. We were just inching along anyway. And it was not only dark, it was freezing, and it began to snow.

Around nine o'clock we finally reached a place where the gorge opened up just enough for a military guard post and where we could

Where our bus convoy spent the night

park far enough from the cliffs so we wouldn't have to worry about being crushed by a boulder during the night. And that was where we spent the night, in the bus, shivering and wondering if we would ever see the dawn. Finn and I couldn't feel our toes, and we hadn't eaten all day. At least the two of us were able to share the huge coat Finn had purchased at the Mongol trading post on the Bayanbulak Plateau. We were grateful it had the whole sheep sewn inside it. But even beneath our sheep, we shivered all night. And it was a long night.

As soon as there was a glimmer of gold on the cliffs on the other side of the gorge, a few Pakistanis went outside and gathered some brush from along the river. Before long, they had a fire going. One by one the rest of us struggled out of our seats and into the frigid morning air to warm our frostbitten toes. Sometime during the night the snow stopped falling, and the sky cleared.

About the time everyone was standing outside wondering what was next, the Chinese official in charge of our convoy asked me to tell the Pakistanis that the road ahead was impassable. He was turning the convoy around and heading back to the Chinese border. I reluctantly relayed his message in English, and my English was rendered into Urdu. The drivers then started up their engines. But the Pakistanis were furious. They weren't about to go back to China. And they made it clear they—not the official—were in charge of the situation. They put rocks in front of all the bus wheels and refused to stand clear. The official wasn't ready for this. This would have never happened in China, with Chinese passengers. Who did these Pakistanis think they were? This was mutiny. It was a standoff is what it was. And the official blinked first.

Once he realized the untenable nature of his position, he told the drivers to turn off their engines, and the mutineers cheered. Then we all gathered back around the brushwood fires and warmed ourselves with hot tea and fried naan. It was our first meal since leaving Tashkorgan and was supplied by our Pakistani busmates. Afterwards, we returned to the work of clearing the road. But this time, we weren't alone. The Pakistani soldiers stationed inside the guardhouse joined us, and they had dynamite. Whenever we came to a boulder too big to budge, we crouched down and covered our ears, while they blew it to smithereens. They said they hadn't bothered doing this earlier because no vehicles had ventured into Pakistan from China for over a month.

And so we proceeded down the Khunjerab Gorge, clearing the road as we went. Around noon we blew our way past the Pakistani military camp at Dih and continued another six kilometers to where the road finally ceased to exist. This was where the American girl had died a few days earlier. She was walking across the slide that had erased the road with several friends when a boulder came careening down the mountain. Her friends jumped out of the way, but she froze. The boulder hit her in the chest, and she died instantly.

The slide was so extensive, the only way forward was to leave our buses behind, cross the gorge on a log bridge, hike over a mountain, re-cross the gorge downstream, and rejoin the road on the other side of the slide. Several dozen men from nearby mountain villages were waiting to help passengers with their luggage. They were asking 300 rupees, or $15, to carry two bags.

End of the line for the Great Kashgar Bus Convoy

Finn and I demurred and strapped on our rucksacks and tiptoed across the "bridge." It consisted of a series of logs lashed together and a guide wire to hold onto. It looked more dangerous than it was. Once across, we started up one of the steepest slopes either of us had ever tried to climb. For every two steps forward, we slid back one step, sending dirt and rocks into the faces of those unlucky enough to be below us. It was slow, arduous going, but we finally made it.

Going down the other side was a lot easier, but re-crossing the gorge wasn't. This time the bridge consisted of a series of wooden planks laid end to end but with no guide wire to hold onto. The Pakistanis in front of us crawled across, and still they almost fell. We had rucksacks strapped to our backs and had no choice but to walk across. As we stepped onto the planks, we could see the water swirling below us. We looked straight ahead and started walking. The last few steps were pure luck, but we didn't argue with luck. We collapsed onto what was left of the road and congratulated ourselves on getting past one more obstacle on the Silk Road.

Once we regained our composure, we hiked down the road for two kilometers and over an even bigger slide. On the other side of the second slide there were half a dozen pickup trucks waiting to ferry travelers to the Pakistan border post of Sust another twenty kilometers away. We were so elated at having crossed the Slide of Doom, we decided not to wait for the first pickup to fill up—which might have taken an hour or two considering the speed with which our fellow passengers were conveying their baggage. We agreed to pay the "special booking fee," as they called it, of 200 rupees, or $10. We waved for the driver to take off, and he took us at breakneck speed down what remained of the road to Sust.

Sust was where travelers went through border formalities. Before taking us to find a room for the night, our driver pulled up in front of the immigration office, and we got out. The official in charge was playing bridge outside on the veranda with three other men. After trumping the last trick, he motioned for us to follow him inside. We were too dazed to sit, so we just stood there in front of his desk while he looked at our passports and visas and entered our names in his ledger. Then he stamped our passports and said, "Welcome to Pakistan." We wanted to tell him how glad we were to be there, how much trouble we had endured to be there, but we were simply too tired. All we wanted to do was eat and sleep.

At least the Khunjerab Pass was behind us, and our passports were stamped, and we were not spending the night on the bus but at the Mountain Refuge Hotel, where a double with a hot shower cost 200 rupees. The owner's name was Ibraham, and the hot milk-tea and fried naan and curry he made for us that night was divine.

Afterwards, we slept the sleep of the dead, and we could have slept for days. But we were also anxious to continue, while there was still a road. The next morning, after supplying us with more hot milk-tea, Ibraham arranged a jeep for us and several other survivors of the Great Kashgar Bus Convoy. For 100 rupees, or $5 apiece, the driver took us as far as the next slide—which was another sixty kilometers down the gorge past the village of Gulmit. The river's name, though, had changed. It was now called the Hunza River, in honor of the small mountain kingdom of the same name toward which we now proceeded in pouring rain and heavy fog.

One of the outstanding features of the landscape between Sust and Gulmit is the barrenness of the valleys where the Hunza River opens up enough for the occasional village. Despite its seeming timelessness, the barrenness is recent. Following a severe earthquake in 1974, a series of landslides dammed the Hunza River and resulted in the formation of a huge lake nearly twenty kilometers long. By the time the river finally managed to break through the natural dam that had stemmed its flow, most of the fertile land between Gulmit and Sust that wasn't washed away was buried beneath deep layers of silt and gravel. As we passed the village of Passu, our driver noted that before 1974 there used to be five times as many people living in that part of the valley. The people there used to support themselves from the sale of dried apricots and other fruit. But their orchards were gone. Those who decided to stay managed to eke out a living by providing services to the occasional

Fellow passengers working their way across rock slides

groups of travelers who came to explore the surrounding peaks and glaciers of the Karakorums. If you liked to hike, Passu was supposedly the place with the best hikes and the best guides. But we didn't stop to find out. We had a date with a six-kilometer-long landslide south of Gulmit that offered as much hiking as we were up for. Two hours after leaving Sust, we were there. We weren't looking forward to working our way across another long slide in the pouring rain, but we had no choice. Then, just as we arrived, the sky opened up and the day went from dismal to glorious.

Back when there were still dinosaurs on Earth, a huge piece of the primordial continent of Gondwanaland broke off and started migrating across the planet. Seventy million years ago, it collided with the Asian Plate, and its northern edge slipped beneath the Asian Plate's southern edge and began lifting it up. The result of that collision—which is still going on—was the formation of the Hindu Kush, the Pamirs, the Himalayas, and the Karakorums, whose stupendous peaks held us spellbound. It was an unforgettable sight: the cataclysmic wreckage of the Earth's greatest traffic accident.

But we didn't let it hold us spellbound long. We waved good-bye to our driver and began negotiating the boulders that made up the slide. We hadn't gone more than fifty meters when we heard a loud crash behind us. We turned and saw a column of dust rising where we had been standing when we waved to our driver. Fortunately for us, we've never been guilty of prolonged good-byes.

Finn and I continued on, invincible in the midday sun. Our near deaths notwithstanding, it was a beautiful day. Meanwhile, we worked our way through the odd pile of rubble and detoured down into the gorge and back up to the road again. We finally caught up to a group of Pakistanis who were also part of the Great Kashgar Bus Convoy. They had hired local porters to carry most of their luggage, but they each had a bundle or two on their own backs. We all stopped to catch our breaths and reminisce about the three days and two nights we spent together.

They asked us if we had any more brandy. I reached into my pack and produced what was left of my last bottle. But they didn't want any. Pakistanis are Muslims, and they don't drink anything stronger than lemonade. They just wanted to see for themselves the cause of our good humor during our long ordeal. We shared a few laughs then waved good-bye. Two hours later, we reached the end of the slide. Several bulldozers were at work, and the Pakistani soldiers in charge said they expected to reopen the road in a couple of days. If they had seen the slides we had to negotiate on our way there, they would have realized they had months, maybe years, of work ahead of themselves, not days.

Finn and I didn't linger. We climbed aboard one of the small vans waiting beyond the bulldozers and didn't even bother asking how far it was to the next slide. We were making progress, and that was good enough. But we couldn't help wonder how the bulldozers got there, and we asked our driver. He said that the road to the south had been cleared. It turned out there was no next slide. The driver was also a surprise. He was blue-eyed and fair-skinned. He said he was from the Hunza Valley. When we asked him about his eyes and complexion, he said his ancestors had come there over 2,000 years ago. They were the remnant

Hunza Valley with Karimabad on the right

forces of Alexander the Great, who marched across the plains south of the Karakorums in the fourth century BC.

Less than an hour later, we were there, in the Hunza Valley. Just past the village of Ganesh, our driver turned onto a road that snaked up a hillside to the village of Karimabad. Karimabad, he said, was where most travelers stayed who came to the valley. It didn't matter to us where we stayed. We were glad to be staying anywhere, anywhere other than a bus. Our driver dropped us off at the Park Hotel, which looked like a European pension. There were no other guests, and the owner showed us the best room in the place. It was spotless, and the beds were like clouds, and there were two huge windows. We opened one of them and beheld the incredible form of Ultar Peak. At 7,400 meters, it was 1,400 meters short of Everest. But unlike Everest, Ultar had never been climbed. It looked like a white diamond set in a ring of clouds. Then we opened the room's other window and beheld a garden of fruit trees and flowers and, briefly, the owner's unmarried daughter washing clothes.

View of Ultar Peak from our hotel window

The owner said he normally charged 300 rupees, but since it was the off-season he would only charge us 250, or $12. And that included a big bucket of scalding hot water anytime we wanted it. It wasn't long before we wanted it. And it wasn't long before we wanted food, too. Less than thirty minutes after we asked, the owner led us into the dining room where we were the only diners. We sat at a table big enough for twenty people and dined on stewed lamb and creamed spinach and potato croquettes the like of which neither of us had ever tasted. We felt like we had died and gone to Heaven.

Actually, we were in Heaven, or at least Shangri-la. The Hunza Valley, it turns out, was the place James Hilton had in mind when he wrote his book *Lost Horizon*, in which several Westerners flee a revolution in India and their plane crashes in the mountains, and they make their way to a valley cut off from man's inhumanity to man where people lead long and happy lives. The only question we had after dinner was: if we ever left, could we find our way back?

香格里拉

20. Shangri-la

Humans are so weird. Even in Shangri-la, life has its problems. The inhabitants on the north side of the valley call the place the Hunza Valley, which was where we were staying, while the inhabitants on the south side call it the Nagar Valley. The people on the two sides disagree about more than names. They have been locked in a feud stretching back over three hundred years.

It seems that the mir who ruled all the land on both sides of the Hunza River had two sons, neither of whom liked the other. And when the mir

was on his deathbed, he decided to divide his realm equally between them. One son got all the land on the north side of the river, and the other son got the land on the south side. As soon as their father was dead, one of the brothers murdered the other, and he, in turn, was murdered by the dead brother's son. And the descendants of the two brothers have been carrying on this ancient feud ever since, with murder being the normal means of succession to the control of one side or the other.

Despite their differences, both sides agree on a common ancestry that stretches back far beyond the seventeenth-century mir and his two sons to the people who came here over 2,000 years ago. Exactly who these people were remains a mystery, but some historians agree with our van driver that they were the remnant forces of Alexander the Great, who marched through the plains just south of the Karakorums in the fourth century BC. One look at the blue-eyed, fair-skinned people of Nagar and Hunza, and it's easy to imagine Alexander's soldiers sneaking away from the hot, humid flatlands and discovering the snowcapped peaks and flower-filled valleys of Shangri-la.

But whether it was Greek soldiers or someone else, there wasn't much information about the people who followed the Indus and then the Hunza into the Karakorums, or why they followed the rivers up that high. Undoubtedly their reasons had something to do with escaping the mosquito-and-tiger-and-man-infested floodplains. Earlier, just before our minivan arrived in Karimabad, we passed an outcrop of rocks, where the Ministry of Tourism had erected a sign proclaiming these the Sacred Rocks of Hunza. Our driver allowed us to pause long enough to examine some of the drawings carved into their surface.

Along with more recent graffiti, historians had identified scenes from local legends and events stretching back more than 2,000 years, including writing said to have been carved into the rocks by the evil cannibal king Shiri Badat with his bare fingers. Shiri Badat was so evil, even his own daughter turned against him. She conspired with her father's enemies, and he fell into a pit they had covered with carpets. Before the king could escape, they filled the pit with wood and set it on fire. The villagers of the Hunza Valley still make bonfires on the winter solstice to celebrate his death. And they dance and slaughter goats. The story was somewhere on those rocks, but the only part we could make out was the part about the goats.

Meanwhile, we woke up in Shangri-la the next morning just as the first light of dawn turned the snowcapped peaks on either side of the valley pink then gold. When the sun finally climbed over the range of peaks to the east, we got up and walked inside the Park Hotel restaurant. Our breakfast was waiting: a large pot of coffee and all the homemade bread and homemade apricot jam we could eat. The owner said the Hunza Valley was as high as apricots grew—any higher and there wouldn't be enough oxygen. The average elevation of the villages in the valley was 2,500 meters, or 8,000 feet. The valley was also famous for the number of people who live to be a hundred, and many of them attribute their longevity to the apricots. We piled on the jam and added a couple more years to our lives.

The owner said we were his first guests since the road to the south had reopened. He said not long after landslides closed the road, the Army evacuated everyone but residents by helicopter. In the course of four days, they evacuated more than 250 tourists. The helicopters landed just above the hotel at the home of the mir. The owner said he used to work for the mir, and the mir rewarded his years of faithful service with the piece of land on which he built his hotel.

Even in Shangri-la visitors need money, and it was time for us to cash some traveler's checks. The owner of our hotel said the local branch of the Bank of Pakistan was right down the road, and after breakfast we walked down the road, and up the road, and down the road looking for it. Finally, with the help of some children, we found it in an alley. The sign outside was missing most of its letters, which was part of the reason we hadn't noticed it. Also, it consisted of little more than one small room with two large desks. And behind the desks sat the two men who managed the place. An Austrian traveler was sitting in a chair in front of one of the desks, and we sat down in front of the other desk. The man behind our desk told us he had a sore throat and asked us what he should take for it. Then he proceeded to question us about visas—visas to anywhere, then about finding a wife.

Trying to cash traveler's checks in Karimabad

Meanwhile, the other man was looking at a traveler's check the Austrian had just signed. He looked at the check and asked to see the Austrian's passport. Then he looked back at the check. It was as if he was carrying on a conversation with the check and the passport, and the conversation went on and on. Finally, he handed back the check and said he couldn't cash it. The Austrian was naturally perplexed. He asked, "Why not?" The man said, "The signatures are different." We peered over the Austrian's shoulder. They looked the same to us. But the man waved the Austrian away and said, "Next." We signed our names with great care and handed him our checks. "Sorry," he said, "We don't have any money today. How about some tea?"

That was our first experience with Pakistani bureaucracy, and we lingered long enough to broaden our knowledge. One of the men clapped his hands, and a few seconds later a young boy entered the room with a tray of cups and a bowl of sugar and a pot of milk and another of tea.

"You're in the Hunza Valley," the man said. "You know what that means? Hunza was named after the Huns. The Huns came here from

China on their way to India in the fifth century, and some of them stayed. That's why we look different from other Pakistanis. And that's why this place is called Hunza."

We asked what Karimabad meant. "That's different. That has nothing to do with the Huns. 'Bad' means 'village.' And 'Karim' is the name Muslims give to one of the aspects of the divine: the maternal aspect, compassion and love. Do you know about love? I don't. I'm a virgin. I'm twenty-eight, and I've never been married. I've never even had a girlfriend. Maybe you could introduce me to a girl in your country. I'd like to find out about love. Here it's so hard." I remembered a bumper sticker a previous visitor had left on our bed at the border post of Sust. It said I DON'T NEED A LOT OF LOVE, JUST A STEADY SUPPLY. Alas, this poor chap had no supply at all, steady or otherwise. But what can you say to someone else about love when you don't understand it yourself? We finished our tea and thanked our lovesick hosts, and returned to the incredible views that greeted us again outside.

Many visitors who come to the Hunza Valley come to climb its mountains. In addition to the unclimbed icy pyramid of Ultar Peak looming directly behind Karimabad, they come to test themselves on the huge white pinnacle of Rakaposhi, directly across from Karimabad on the south side of the valley. Rakaposhi is 7,800 meters high, and unlike Ultar it has been climbed. And to the east of Rakaposhi on the same snowcovered spine is Diran Peak. At 7,300 meters, Diran isn't as high as Rakaposhi, but it has claimed more lives than any mountain in Pakistan. Local guides call it "ghost mountain."

Even if visitors aren't up to mounting an expedition to the peaks, they can visit the base camps other climbers have used for their ascents—successful or otherwise. In the case of Rakaposhi and Diran, the normal route is to continue down the Karakorum Highway to a place where the road crosses the Hunza River. On the other side, a jeep track leads to the village of Minapin. The trail to both peaks starts right behind the village's only hostel. It's a seven-hour hike to the main base camp and another hour beyond that to a huge meadow that stretches below both peaks. Visitors who plan to make it into more than a day trip—and

View of Rakaposhi from Karimabad

the meadow is at least a two-day trip—can hire guides and gear in the village. But even with guides and all the right gear, it's said to be windy and cold, except during the height of summer. Fortunately, it was late fall, and that was all the excuse we needed to retire to the garden of the Park Hotel, where we wrote postcards and caught the occasional glimpse of the owner's lovely daughter in her silken sari and head scarf hanging up our clothes—which we were suddenly too lazy to wash now that we were in Shangri-la.

As far as I've been able to figure out, soon after they're born, Pakistani women have devices implanted in their heads that warn them whenever a man so much as looks at them. In this case, the owner's daughter hadn't even finished hanging up our clothes when her alarm went off, and she disappeared into the part of the hotel reserved for women. Her mother had to come outside and finish the job. Pakistan is a Muslim country. In fact, that is why it existed in the first place, partitioned from India to provide the subcontinent's Muslims with their own state. The essence of the Islamic religion, to which all Muslims adhere, is to surrender to God's Will, although apparently women surrender a little more than men.

In the area of Pakistan where we had been traveling so far, most people were members of the Ismaili branch of the Shiite sect of Islam. The Shiites trace their religious ancestry to Muhammad's son-in-law, Ali, who was more interested in religious practice than power politics but who still got himself assassinated. A hundred years later, the Ismailis split with the Shiites during another dispute over practice, and they have been a separate sect ever since, with their own leader being the Aga Khan, the forty-ninth successor of the man who started the Ismaili sect. We were told that the beautiful stone building at the west end of the valley was the school he built for the village girls. We tried not to look at it too long.

Finn and I spent the whole day doing nothing more than recuperating in Karimabad. We even took naps. It was almost like we were on vacation. But we weren't on vacation, and it was time to continue down the road, while it was still open. Before we left the next morning, the owner of our hotel asked us to sign his guest register. We flipped through and read this poem penned by a British traveler in 1988:

> *Far from the madding crowd's ignoble strife*
> *here in the land of apricots and long life*
> *amid ice springs of water the peaks stand stark*
> *over a kingdom of green and here at the Park*
> *hospitable haven below the fort*
> *we stopped awhile, too short, too short*

I almost forgot the fort, Baltit Fort. As the poem said, it was above the hotel and overlooked the whole valley, and no visit to Karimabad was complete without at least a nod in its direction. The fort was built some five hundred years ago by the local mir for a princess from the Tibetan kingdom of Baltistan east of Gilgit, hence its name: Baltit Fort. The princess not only gave the fort its name, she also brought her own artisans and gave the fort its distinctive Tibetan-style architecture. The fort had seen better days, but at least it was being renovated. Meanwhile, the local mir had moved out and relocated in more modern quarters just above the Park, where we dashed off a less memorable entry than the one above and proceeded to our next destination, the town of Gilgit—an actual town—and where, we hoped, we would find an actual functioning branch of the Bank of Pakistan.

吉尔吉特

21. Gilgit

B EFORE THE KARAKORUM HIGHWAY was built, the eighty-kilo-
meter trip from the Hunza Valley to Gilgit took seven hours in a
jeep. A jeep was still the way to go when we were there, especially since
there had been more landslides, but the trip now took only three hours.
It was with relief that we arrived in Gilgit and checked into the Chinar
Inn, the second most expensive place in town. The reason we chose the
Chinar was that it was operated by the Pakistan Tourist Development
Corporation, and it just so happened that the Pakistan Tourist Develop-

ment Corporation, better known as PTDC, was in charge of dispensing the foreign traveler quota on the daily flight from Gilgit to Islamabad, with two seats going to the lucky foreigners. The alternative was a fourteen-hour bus ride, assuming the road was open.

To qualify for the drawing, we had to pay 600 rupees, or more than $20, for a room at the Chinar. But that included a big bathtub we could fill with cold water whenever we liked. Plus, the rooms were all set around a spacious lawn. And there was a Star-TV hookup in the hotel lobby. So we signed our names in the register and conveyed our request for two seats on the next flight to Islamabad. The manager seemed not to hear us. He wanted to know if we had just come from Islamabad. "No," we said, "we've come from Kashgar." "Kashgar? How could you come from Kashgar? The road has been closed for more than a month now." When we insisted that such was the case, he opened a drawer and produced a sheet of paper. He asked us if we knew Marcie Nelson. No. Who was Marcie Nelson? He showed us the paper. It was a coroner's report: Marcie Nelson, age twenty-four, American, place of death: Khunjerab Pass, cause of death: boulder in the chest.

"You came through the Khunjerab Pass?" "Yes. We came through the Khunjerab Pass, and we would like two seats on the next plane out of here." The manager finally realized we were serious and proceeded to take our money and put our names on the list for the daily flight. He even proceeded to cash our traveler's checks without checking our signatures or asking any questions about love.

Gilgit was Pakistan's equivalent of Kashgar, a hub where various spokes of the Silk Road have met since ancient times. Nowadays, it is the administrative center for what the Pakistan government calls its Northern Areas. In 1947, when the British government decided to split its former subcontinental empire into separate Muslim and Hindu states—namely East and West Pakistan for Muslims and India for Hindus—the dozens of principalities in the Hindu Kush, the Karakorums, and the Himalayas were classified as independent and not part of the agreement.

Gilgit traditionally allied itself with Kashmir, which had a largely Muslim population but a Hindu ruler. And when the ruler decided to

Finn and author outside the Chinar Inn with friend from Karimabad

side with India, this did not go down well in Pakistan. Before the ink had dried, the blood began to flow, and it flowed for two years until 1949, when the United Nations managed to convince both sides to stop fighting and split the territory under dispute. For its part, Pakistan received a small slice of Kashmir and the 70,000 square kilometers of territory in its Northern Areas.

The Northern Areas, though, were not as important as Kashmir, and Pakistan has continued to try to liberate its fellow Muslims there. War broke out again in 1965. Six years later, when fighting stopped, Pakistan not only had not gained any territory, its eastern half (namely, East Pakistan) had seceded to become Bangladesh. Meanwhile, the Northern Areas remained in limbo. If Pakistan made them into a regular province, that would be tantamount to agreeing to the partition of Kashmir. And so there they were, and us too, in limbo.

The hotel manager said flying out the next day was out of the question, but he thought he could get us seats in another day or two. So there was no sense in being in a hurry. After dropping our bags in our room, we ordered a pot of tea and sat on the veranda and let our gaze wander up the Gilgit Valley. Up the same valley in the summer of 1870, an Englishman named George Hayward was kneeling in the early morning sun, watching its light illuminate the peaks for the last time. A few months earlier, Hayward had been informed by the Royal Geographic Society that he had been awarded their Gold Medal for his explorations in the Karakorums and the Pamirs.

Back in the nineteenth century, the Royal Geographic Society's Gold Medal was the highest honor an explorer could receive. In the Society's hallowed halls, Hayward's portrait still hangs next to that of Samuel Baker, explorer of the Nile, and directly across from another Gold Medal winner, Sir H. M. Stanley, who met Dr. Livingstone in Africa, I presume. During Hayward's explorations, he learned of a campaign of genocide being conducted against some of the tribes around Gilgit by the Maharaja of Kashmir, and he published an account of one such foul deed wherein the Maharaja's soldiers were reported to have tossed babies into the air and cut them in two before they fell. Needless to say, release of the news infuriated the Maharaja. Before Hayward could leave the Karakorums, he found himself kneeling in the first light of dawn, awaiting his execution. His grave is somewhere in the old British cemetery in Gilgit. Meanwhile, we turned our attention to more pleasant matters and poured ourselves another cup of tea.

After considering the possibilities, we finally decided on an excursion to the countryside. Through the good offices of a young lad whom we had met earlier in the Hunza Valley, we hired a jeep and proceeded into the Gilgit Valley, the same valley where George Hayward paid with his life during his exploration of the source of the Oxus River. Our goal was more modest. We drove six kilometers west of Gilgit up a winding, sometimes asphalt road to the mouth of a gorge called the Kirgah Nullah. On one of the cliff faces someone had carved a large statue of the Buddha. Nobody seemed to know when it was carved or who carved it. Buddhism disappeared in this region a thousand years ago, so it must have been carved well before that. As far as local villagers were

Buddha statue on the cliffs above Kirgah Nullah Gorge

concerned, the statue wasn't a buddha. It was a man-eating giant who terrorized the valley until a Muslim holy man pinned it to the cliff.

The carving wasn't especially artistic, and the statue was only four or five meters high, but it was just about the only evidence that Buddhism had ever flourished in this Muslim land. The only other evidence was across the valley above the village of Naupur less than a kilometer away. In 1931, someone found a cache of birch-bark manuscripts entombed inside an ancient stupa. The materials have since become known among Sanskrit scholars as the Gilgit Manuscripts, and they include the Sanskrit versions of many Buddhist scriptures of which there are no longer any other copies.

With the help of the village constable, we managed to find the stupa site, but there wasn't much left to see. More interesting was the sound the wind made coming down the valley. We hoped it was promising to fly us out of there. Having nothing else to do, we returned to Gilgit and our hotel. It was too late in the year to climb mountains and a bit too early for Gilgit's famous weeklong no-rules polo competition. Indeed, polo, the game played on horseback where riders knock a ball around a grass-covered pitch while spectators make remarks about the weather instead of the moral qualities of the participants.

But in Gilgit polo is a bit different, as it should be. After all, polo originated in Central Asia, not in the British Isles. It was first developed into a competitive sport by the Persians, on the other side of the Hindu Kush. For reasons no one could explain, polo, as played in Pakistan's Northern Areas, had become the wildest, most unbridled form of the sport anywhere. One travel guide noted that "the unbelievable daredevil horsemanship of the players was almost matched by the bravery of the spectators who lined the ground atop a low wall from which the ball caromed off at amazing speeds." Also noteworthy was that the pace of the game was controlled by a military band of drums and clarinets that increased the tempo and pitch of its music as the game progressed. The speed with which the game was played made great demands not only on the players and the spectators but on the horses as well. To make sure they were up to it, they were fed a diet consisting largely of walnuts and

View of Himalayas during flight from Gilgit

mulberries—the horses, not the players or spectators. The weeklong competition is held in late March and again in early November. But it was October, and we were more interested in plane tickets.

And we were in luck. Upon returning to our hotel, the manager had good news. He said we were booked on the flight to Islamabad the next morning, weather permitting, and he gave us a letter to take to the local airline office authorizing us to have our names added to the passenger list. As in India, Pakistan had instituted a foreign traveler quota on its government-operated airplanes and trains. And by wisely paying the high room rate at the Chinar Inn, we had qualified for the two seats available to foreigners on the next day's flight to the capital.

The Lonely Planet travel guide to the Karakorum Highway called the flight "one of the most spectacular civil air routes in the world," the reason being that passengers fly in a small propeller-driven aircraft over the outstretched western edge of the Himalayas and the awesome shoulders of Nanga Parbat, which at 8,100 meters is the eighth-highest mountain in the world. If the weather isn't perfect, the plane doesn't fly. And if the plane doesn't fly, the remaining option is a fourteen-hour assault to one's butt and nerves aboard one of the daily buses winding its way to Islamabad along the final section of the Karakorum Highway beside the Indus River. After leaving the west slope of Mount Kailash in Tibet, the Indus skirts the entire Himalayan chain and enters the Hunza River just south of Gilgit—at which point it turns south for Islamabad, Mohenjo-daro, and the Arabian Sea. We hoped to see it from higher up than a bus window.

When we went to the airline office to add our names to the list of passengers for the next day's flight, we were told the plane hadn't flown for three days due to nothing more than the presence of a few clouds in the sky. Later that night it rained. As we listened to the sound outside our window, we sighed, then rolled over and went to sleep. When we woke the next morning, there wasn't a wisp of white in the sky. We enjoyed a final pot of tea on the veranda and proceeded to the airport, which was at the east edge of town and actually within walking distance of our hotel.

The plane landed shortly before noon. It was a forty-passenger Fokker Friendship, and it didn't even bother shutting down its engines. As soon as the passengers from Islamabad disembarked, we took their places on board. And as soon as their luggage was off the plane, and ours was loaded, we roared down the runway and climbed to a cruising altitude of just under 5,000 meters, or 16,000 feet.

As soon as we were airborne, Finn and I slipped our batteries back into our cameras and began transferring Nanga Parbat's 8,100-meter image to celluloid. We had to take the batteries out and hide them when we went through airport security, otherwise they would have been confiscated. I'm not saying where I hid mine. Over the next hour, I shot up two rolls of film. Even through foggy windows the prints were spectacular. We flew over the roof of the world at a cost of a mere 600 rupees or less than $25. But, of course, it all depended on the weather. We heard later that the plane didn't fly again for another three days.

伊斯蘭堡

22. Islamabad

DOWN WE CAME DOWN INTO THE HOT, humid plains watered by the mighty Indus, the same river we left earlier that morning shortly after taking off from Gilgit. The Indus flows all the way through Pakistan, from its northern border with China to its southern border on the Arabian Sea. Bounded by the Great Indian Desert to the east and the Hindu Kush to the west, the Indus is Pakistan. Five thousand years ago, its watershed was also the scene of one of the world's first civilizations. When I was in school, we called it the Indus Valley civilization, in con-

trast with civilizations that developed around the same time along other rivers: the Tigris and Euphrates of Mesopotamia, the Nile of Egypt, and the Yellow River of China. Nowadays, archaeologists prefer to call it the Harappa Culture after the ancient city of the same name they discovered near Lahore in the 1920s.

Harappa Culture included a number of urban centers in the Indus floodplain, including Mohenjo-daro, and developed in response to the accumulation of surplus wealth due to innovations in agriculture and animal husbandry as well as to the control of trade routes leading west toward the Mediterranean, east toward India, and north toward Central Asia and China. Unfortunately, the ruins of Mohenjo-daro and other Harappa sites weren't on our itinerary. We only planned to stay in Islamabad long enough to find a way back to where we began our journey, namely Hong Kong.

When Pakistan first became an independent state in 1947, its capital was located in Karachi at the southern end of the country, where the Indus emptied into the Arabian Sea. But the huge influx of Muslim refugees that followed the partition from India soon swelled that city beyond its means. There was such a shortage of housing, civil servants had to sleep in tents in city parks. The government's solution was to begin construction of a new capital at the northern end of the country, where the Indus left the mountains and began its pilgrimage toward Mecca. The choice of a site at the northern end of the country also had something to do with the government's relationship with its military, which was headquartered in Rawalpindi.

Islamabad and Rawalpindi are only fifteen kilometers from each other, but they couldn't be more different. Islamabad is a planned city with wide tree-lined streets and the feel of a Western suburb. In short, a boring place to visit. Rawalpindi, meanwhile, is crowded, noisy and centered around a series of bazaars. The exception is the "cantonment" around which Pindi, as it was called, first developed. The cantonment was one of Britain's gifts to the subcontinent. It consisted of the administrative and residential parts of a military base and was established outside urban areas. In the case of Rawalpindi, the cantonment was

Indus River flowing out of the Himalayas

established in the 1840s following Britain's conclusion of its war against the Sikhs. The English made it into their largest such base in Asia. Following the departure of British forces, the Pakistani Army moved in, and it is no secret that Rawalpindi is the real center of power in Pakistan, not Islamabad. Naturally, we decided to stay in Pindi.

After we collected our bags, we jumped into a taxi, traveled down Airport Road into Rawalpindi, turned onto the Mall, passed the President's residence, and checked into the venerable but deteriorating Flashman's Hotel. As always, we made our first order of business arranging transportation to our next destination, which was Hong Kong and home. The plants, I imagined, had died, and I would need to buy new ones.

Finn and I visited several travel agents within walking distance of our hotel, and they were all quite willing to sell us tickets. But none of them could get us a reservation until the following week, or just in time for me to get fired. Then I remembered a sign we had seen at our hotel in Gilgit: FOR TOP, NUMBER-ONE TRAVEL SERVICE, NOBODY BEATS SITARA TRAVEL. So we tried Sitara. Sure enough, they got us reservations when no one else could. Ironically, Sitara was also responsible for chartering a Pakistan Airline Boeing 707 to pick up the Pakistanis still stranded in China—a flight that took place while we were still negotiating the landslides that closed the Karakorum Highway.

With tickets in our pockets, we proceeded to our next order of business: cold beer. We continued down the street and entered the lobby of the ultra-fancy, way-beyond-our-means Pearl Continental Hotel and asked where the bar was. Up until then we had survived on Chinese brandy. But our supply had run out in the Hunza Valley. "Sorry, Sir, you're in Pakistan," the man behind the counter said. "No alcohol in public. Go back to your own hotel and drink in your room." It is illegal for Pakistanis to drink any kind of alcohol, and foreigners were only allowed to drink in the privacy of their homes or their hotel rooms. Back at the Flashman, we were directed to another wing of the hotel, where we knocked on a window. A man inside opened it and asked to see our passports. Then he asked us to sign a register and pay for our purchase: six bottles of Murree Beer. We felt like we were doing something illegal, as if it was still Prohibition. And so we returned to our room with our beer in a brown paper bag so that no one could see what we had. Once inside, we closed the curtain and opened the first two bottles. The label said 125 YEARS OF FINE BREWING. We wondered how such a company had managed to stay in business in a land where it was illegal to drink beer. We didn't wonder long. We were just glad it had. Then we turned on the TV. If you have ever wondered what happened to those programs that never made it onto TV in the West, or if they did it wasn't for long, wonder no more. We watched something called *Nashville Grab*, in which some handsome yokels and bounteous belles ran around Nashville trying to get their big break in country music.

Although we had managed to get reservations on a flight to Hong Kong, we still had one more day to kill. There was no way we were going to sit in our room, beer or no beer, and keep watching TV. One night of that was enough. We had to get out and see something. We decided to hire a car and head for the ruins of the ancient kingdom of Gandhara where Mahayana Buddhism is said to have begun. The ruins were just over an hour away down the Grand Trunk Road.

The Grand Trunk Road is over 2,000 years old and was used by the Indians as well as the British to speed the transport of troops between Calcutta and Kabul. Rudyard Kipling called it the backbone of India and compared it to a river: "a river of life such as exists nowhere else in the world, running straight, bearing all castes and all manner of traffic for fifteen hundred miles."

The next morning, we hid our remaining two bottles of beer from the maid and arranged with the hotel bellman for a car to take us to Taxila. Taxila was the ancient capital of Gandhara, which once controlled the area on either side of the Indus where it comes down from the Karakorums and spills out onto the plains. Basically, Gandhara was the ancient version of Pakistan. It also straddled several important trade routes, including those that connected India with Central Asia and the Mediterranean. Over the centuries, the kingdom's rulers included Aryans, Persians, Indians, even Greeks. And its capital was just west of Rawalpindi off the Grand Trunk Road.

Tea time on the Grand Trunk Road

Once the road left the city, it led into the Margalla Hills and through the Margalla Pass. The Pass wasn't that impressive, little more than a short slice through some rocks. The only thing of note was a large obelisk on a hill near the road erected as a memorial to John Nicholson, a British general who died fighting the Sikhs in 1857. According to our guidebook there was an inscription on the obelisk that read "He was mourned by both sides with equal grief." Apparently, it wasn't an idle exaggeration: he left behind a group of Sikh followers who still call themselves Nikalsenis in his honor. We considered stopping, but our driver suggested there was a better place.

Just beyond the pass, we pulled over to the side of the road and stopped for a pot of tea under an open-air lean-to. Indeed, it was a better place. But it was an odd place. There were tables, but no chairs, only cots. And there were no mattresses on the cots, only the ropes that held them together. This was where truck drivers stopped to sleep off the effects of the long haul between Afghanistan and India, and there were half a dozen drivers in various degrees of sleep or stupefaction. In addition to dispensing tea, the proprietors also dispensed hashish.

Trucks on the Grand Trunk Road

Of course, hashish was illegal, but our driver said the Margalla Pass was beyond government control, and people did pretty much as they pleased. Naturally, we chose tea.

While Finn and I sipped our brew, to which we followed the custom prevalent throughout the subcontinent of adding milk and sugar, our driver said this was the same pass used by Babur when he invaded India in the sixteenth century. Babur was born with the royal blood of Tamerlane coursing through his veins. Finn and I had visited Tamerlane's tomb during our stop in Yining. At the end of the fourteenth century, Tamerlane swept down from his home in Uzbekistan and wreaked havoc in India, and Babur decided to follow in the footsteps of his noble ancestor. After he was kicked out of his own kingdom by his fellow Uzbeks, Babur captured Kabul when he was only twenty-one. He then headed east through the Margalla Pass, right past where we were drinking tea, and into the Panjab and across all of India. Even a cavalry force of a thousand elephants didn't stand a chance against his guns. Yes, guns. It was the first time anyone in Northern India had seen such weapons.

Thus began one of the most glorious cultural periods in the history of the subcontinent: the Mughal dynasty.

Babur wasn't simply a conqueror, he was also a writer, and he left behind an autobiography in which he clearly pined for his homeland: "Hindustan," he wrote, "is a country of few charms. Its people have no good looks; of genius and capacity none; of manners none; there are no good horses, no good dogs, no grapes, muskmelons, or first rate fruits, no ice or cold water, no good bread, and no hot baths. But it has," he went on, "masses of gold and silver." Unfortunately, he didn't live long enough to enjoy his gold or silver. When his son fell ill, Babur offered Allah his own life in exchange. His wish was granted, and his son recovered. But his son was forced to yield control of the empire to the rebel chieftain Sher Shah, who embarked on a great building program that included major portions of the Grand Trunk Road—where we ordered another pot of tea.

Five years later, Sher Shah died, and Babur's son came to power. But less than seven months later, he fell down the steps of his library and broke his neck. He was then succeeded by his son, whose name was Akbar. Akbar was one of the greatest rulers in the history of the subcontinent. He was as wise as he was powerful, and he often disguised himself and ventured into villages to see how people really lived.

On one such occasion, he heard a song about a lady named Rupmati who was in the harem of Baz Bahadar, ruler of Malwa. Akbar was so overcome by the words of the song, he grew jealous, and he sent an army against Baz Bahadar. When Baz Bahadar was defeated and fled for his life, Akbar's soldiers entered Baz Bahadar's harem just in time to see the beautiful Rupmati swallow a vial of poison and die. Akbar nearly died of grief. Romance, it seemed, played a large part in the lives of the Mughal emperors. Akbar's grandson was so in love with one of his wives, he built the Taj Mahal in her memory. More tea, anyone?

One story I haven't told until now was how Pakistan came to be. Its existence, alas, is inextricably tied to the mutual mistrust and oppression between the subcontinent's Muslims and Hindus. While Hinduism has been the dominant religion for thousands of years, Islam didn't enter India until the seventh century—not long after Muhammad's death. But it wasn't until the Mughal dynasty of the sixteenth century that Muslim rulers controlled enough of the subcontinent to ensure the spread of their religion at all levels and in all places. Ever since then, religious affiliation has been used in the subcontinent by those who struggle for power to rally support. And each side can point to countless massacres and foul deeds in that struggle, the list of which continues to grow even today.

In modern times, among those who ended up working for a separate Muslim state instead of a unified India was Mohammed Ali Jinnah. In the beginning, Jinnah worked with Gandhi in the fight for independence from the British. But Jinnah soon realized that neither Gandhi nor any other Hindu politician was willing to guarantee Muslims their fair share of power in a new, independent India. When Gandhi's Congress Party refused to include members of Jinnah's Muslim League in the government being formed to take over from the British, violence erupted. In Calcutta, 5,000 people were killed in three days. The man in charge of handing over power at that time was Lord Mountbatten, and to prevent further bloodshed he gave Jinnah his Pakistan: where the P stood for the northern province of Panjab, the A for Afghanistan (watch out, Afghanistan), the K for Kashmir, the S for the southern province of Sind, and the Stan is Persian for "land." Together the letters mean "land of the pure" in Urdu. And with that, we were finally out of tea.

As Finn and I got up to leave, we walked past dozens of truck drivers trying to revive themselves with tea or to stupefy themselves with hashish. Their vehicles were all parked right outside, and it was the first chance we had to examine these works of art at close quarters. For foreign travelers like ourselves, the first thing we noticed on the way from the airport to our hotel was that every commercial vehicle was a rolling collection of kitsch. Trucks, buses, taxis, even rickshaws were covered with paintings and trinkets from stem to stern. As far as we could determine, Hieronymus Bosch had been forced to return to Earth to atone for his grotesque creations and was currently living and working here in Pakistan.

Buddhist ruins at Taxila

Every subject imaginable was grist for Pakistan's vehicle artists: scenes from nature, scenes from the farm, scenes from movies, scenes from the life of Muhammad—especially his ascension to Heaven on the wings of a creature that was half-woman and half-horse. In addition to covering every inch of their vehicles' surfaces with paintings, drivers festooned their pride-and-joys with tinkling chains of tin, plastic flowers, mud-flaps that belonged in museums of the bizarre, and chintz of every conceivable material, color, and form. One could only imagine the loss to the art world every traffic accident entailed.

Once we satisfied our artistic curiosities, we resumed our journey, feeling very embarrassed in our very plain Toyota sedan. At least we didn't have far to go. Little more than an hour after leaving our hotel, we arrived at the ruins of Taxila. This ancient capital of Gandhara was ruled in turn by Aryans, Persians, Greeks, Indians, Scythians, Parthians, Kushans, and finally by Huns, who consigned Gandhara to the dustbin of history in the fifth century AD. And in the dustbin it stayed until the first half of the twentieth century, when the Englishman John Marshall

Buddhist ruins at Taxila

began a series of excavations that made Taxila one of the most important archaeological sites in all of Asia.

According to the *Ramayana* of the Hindus, the kingdom of Gandhara was founded by Bharata, the younger brother of Rama, and Taxila was founded by one of Bharata's sons, Taksha, the serpent prince—which would put the founding of the city somewhere in the second millennium BC. The Jains put it back even further, claiming it was visited by Rishabha, the legendary founder of their religion, millions of years ago.

According to Marshall, "the truth disclosed by the hard facts of excavation is much more sober." The earliest remains uncovered so far date back no more than the sixth century BC, when the kingdom was annexed by the Persians to the eastern border of their empire. And in Persian hands it remained until Persia itself was conquered in the fourth century BC by Alexander. To confirm his claim to all Persian territory, Alexander led his forces to Taxila and camped here in 326 BC long enough to hold the usual Greek sacrifices and athletic games and to enjoy the fruits of his recent marriage to the Bactrian beauty, Roxanne.

Alexander's earliest biographer noted that Roxanne was one of the most beautiful women in all of Asia, but she wasn't so beautiful that she distracted Alexander from his self-declared mission of conquering the known world—which didn't include China but did include India. After pausing in Taxila, Alexander continued his eastward march—though not for long. His soldiers soon threatened to mutiny, and he was forced to give up his quest. After leaving Greek officers to administer the newly conquered territories, he headed back to Greece. But halfway home, he died in Babylon in 323 BC.

The officers he left behind didn't last much longer. Four years after Alexander left for Greece, Chandragupta Maurya ascended to the throne of the kingdom of Magadha in the middle reaches of the Ganges at the age of twenty-one. It was a shame that he and Alexander never met. They had so much in common yet represented two of the world's most different civilizations. As Alexander had done in the Mediterranean and Asia Minor in his march eastward, Chandragupta proceeded in a like fashion in his march westward, until he possessed the entire northern half of the subcontinent. In so doing, Chandragupta extended his empire to the very edge of modern Iran—which was ruled by the Greek general Seleucus Nicator. To guard his new empire against Nicator, Chandragupta made Taxila second only to his own capital at Patna. And he made his grandson, Ashoka, Taxila's governor.

Having accomplished as much as he dared hope for in the realm of earthly affairs, Chandragupta converted to Jainism and abdicated in favor of his son to become an ascetic. Together with his teacher, Chandragupta traveled to Southern India, where he ended his life by slow starvation in the orthodox Jain manner. Meanwhile, his son extended the boundaries of the new Mauryan Empire into the southern half of the subcontinent. And Chandragupta's grandson, Ashoka, completed the first unification of the entire Indian subcontinent under one ruler.

As his grandfather had done before him, Ashoka, too, turned to religion after he had sent hundreds of thousands of Indians to their deaths. He suddenly became overcome by the enormity of suffering his conquests had caused. He became a Buddhist and spent the rest of his life

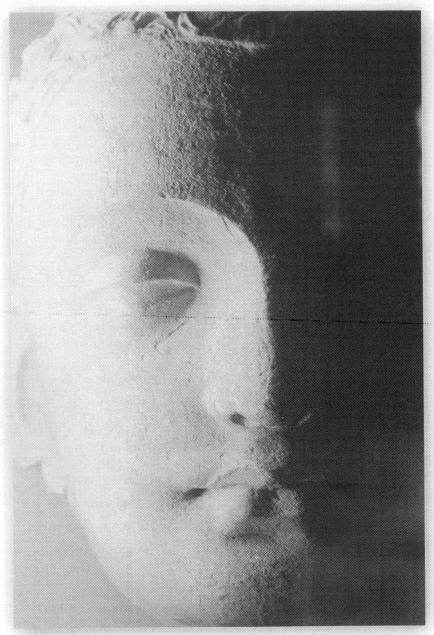

Gandharan sculpture of the Buddha

making known the teachings of his new faith not only throughout India but also in the lands beyond, which he did by erecting thousands of stupas containing portions of the Buddha's remains.

Our first day on the Silk Road, Finn and I visited Famen Temple a hundred kilometers west of Sian. Several years earlier, workers discovered a miniature casket inside the temple's crumbling pagoda containing the Buddha's finger bone. It was a present from Ashoka to the king of China. In the third century BC, the Chou dynasty was still technically in power in China, and the site of Famen Temple was within the precincts of the dynasty's royal burial ground. But despite the early arrival of the Buddha's finger bone, his teachings didn't make any impact in China for several more centuries. Ironically, when they finally did, Taxila and the kingdom of Gandhara played the leading role. But it wasn't the Buddhism of the ascetic wing of the Church that impressed the Chinese.

Not long after Ashoka's death, Gandhara became part of the Greek kingdoms to the west, and Taxila became the major center of learning for a new school of Buddhism: the Mahayana. And it was from Taxila that the new Mahayana branch of Buddhism first spread across Central Asia to China. In our own travels along the Silk Road, we had been following the route of the Chinese monk Hsuan-tsang. When Hsuan-tsang reached Gandhara in the seventh century, he found more than one thousand monasteries in the kingdom. And many of their remains are still visible at Taxila and other sites.

Before proceeding to the ruins themselves, Finn and I began at the museum that housed the collection of artifacts unearthed by John Marshall during the first half of the twentieth century. It was as if we had stumbled by mistake into a museum in Athens. But it was no mistake. Taxila was where East met West.

About the same time that Mahayana Buddhism began developing in India, the Mauryan Empire lost control of its northwest territories to a series of Greek or Greek-related rulers. And when Buddhism began to spread to China along the Central Asian portion of the Silk Road, it was the Greek-inspired Buddhist art of Taxila that arrived in the Middle Kingdom. In fact, it was Taxila and the kingdom of Gandhara that first

Dharmarajika Stupa containing the Buddha's relics

represented the figure of the Buddha. Before that, Buddhists worshipped the image of the bodhi tree under which the Buddha was enlightened or a set of footprints representing the Buddha's departure into the bliss of Nirvana. Taxila, it turned out, was where the Buddha became human again.

Taxila was also the conduit through which most of the other aspects of Indian and Persian culture were transmitted to China. Whether it was in the realms of music, art, or religion, it came from Gandhara and its capital—which was the most cosmopolitan center in the subcontinent, a mixture of Indian, Persian, and even Greek culture.

In addition to the small but excellent museum, we visited several sites in the nearby hills and walked through Taxila's various incarnations, beginning with the Bir site, a few hundred meters from the museum, and ending with the Sirsuk site about two kilometers away, where the Huns put an end to Taxila once and for all in the fifth century, and finally the Mora-du site, which the Huns missed and which still contained the most perfect stupa in that part of Asia.

Our visit coincided with the end of the monsoon season, and all the sites were covered by new grass, with the occasional pile of rubble marking the former existence of a temple or a stupa. By far the biggest pile of rubble, and it wasn't all rubble, was the Dharmarajika Stupa, erected by Ashoka in the third century BC over the relics of the Buddha. Standing in front of the stupa, we realized we had finally reached the end of the line. We had traveled from the ancient capital of China and had arrived at the ancient capital of Northwest India, from where Buddhism spread to China 2,000 years ago along the Silk Road.

After paying our respects, we returned via the Margalla Pass to Rawalpindi and began packing for the trip home. Of course, no trip is quite complete without buying some item to take back home to remind one of the joys and sufferings of the road. Finn and I opted for a visit to one of the carpet merchants just behind our hotel. There were carpets from everywhere: China, Iran, the former Soviet Union, and, of course, Afghanistan. The Afghan carpets, in particular, attracted my attention, especially the new ones with patterns consisting of helicopter gunships and tanks and shoulder-held missile launchers. But in the end, I opted for a traditional Afghan camel hair carpet with stylized flowers. It was red, in case I or one of my guests should spill the odd glass of wine. And the size was just right too: six by four, just big enough for a few folks to sit around and hear about the great trip we took on the Silk Road.

Finn and I weren't too sure what we would remember. No doubt, we'll remember to begin in Sian, the ancient capital of eleven Chinese dynasties; and we'll work our way through a few royal tombs and Buddhist pagodas; and, of course, we'll get sick; and then we'll visit a bunch of Buddhist caves full of statues without heads and paintings of buddhas without eyes; and we'll walk into the dunes; and we'll eat grapes and watch the Uighurs dance; and we'll ride Kazak ponies in the Tienshan Mountains and more buses than we would want to remember; and we'll dodge boulders in the Khunjerab Pass and recuperate in Shangri-la; and we'll pay our respects to the Buddha at Taxila; and then we'll buy a carpet and go home; and when our friends come over to visit, we'll say the magic words that will fly us all back to the Silk Road, just a thought away.

Lexicon

THE FOLLOWING LIST INCLUDES the modified Wade-Giles romanization used throughout this book for Chinese names, places, and terms. In each entry, the Wade-Giles romanization is followed by the Pinyin romanization and the traditional Chinese characters. Although the Wade-Giles system is no longer fashionable, it was designed as a compromise for speakers of various European languages in the mid- and late nineteenth century, while the Pinyin system was designed for Russian speakers in the mid-twentieth century.

WADE-GILES	PINYIN	CHINESE
Abakh	Abake	阿巴克
Aidkah	Aitiduo'er	艾提朵尔
Aitinghu	Aidinghu	艾丁湖
Aksu	Akesu	阿克蘇
Amita	Amida	阿彌陀

Wade-Giles	Pinyin	Chinese
An-la	Anla	安拉
Artush	Atushi	阿圖什
Ashoka	Ayu	阿育
Astana	Asitana	阿斯塔那
Baidan Jaran	Badanjilin	巴丹吉林
Baluka	Balujia	跋祿迦
Bayanbulak	Bayinbuluke	巴音布魯克
Beijing	Beijing	北京
Bezeklik	Bozikeli	柏孜克里
Bogda	Bogeda	博格達
bughra khan	bugelahan	布格拉汗
Chang Ch'ien	Zhang Qian	張騫
Chang San-feng	Chang Sanfeng	張三丰
Chang Ta-ch'ien	Zhang Daqian	張大千

WADE-GILES	PINYIN	CHINESE
Ch'ang-an	Changan	長安
Changyeh	Zhangye	張掖
Chaoerhan	Zhao'erhan	昭尔罕
Chaohuli	Zhaohuli	昭怙厘
Chapchal	Chabucha'er	察布查尔
Chiang Tzu-ya	Jiang Ziya	姜子牙
Chiaoho	Jiaohe	交河
Chiayukuan	Jiayuguan	嘉峪關
Chiehpanto	Jiepantuo	竭盤陀
Chihshan	Zhishan	峙山
Chihshashan	Chishashan	赤沙山
Chilien	Qilian	祁連
Chinchou	Qinzhou	秦州
Chinghai	Qinghai	清海
Chini Bagh	Qini Bage	其尼巴格
Chinling	Qinling	秦嶺

WADE-GILES	PINYIN	CHINESE
Chintai	Jintai	金台
Chiuchuan	Jiuquan	酒泉
Ch'i (lady)	Qi	戚
ch'in	qin	琴
Ch'in (dynasty)	Qin	秦
Ch'ing (dynasty)	Qing	清
Chou (dynasty/duke)	Zhou	周
Chouyuan	Zhouyuan	周原
Chu Teh	Zhu De	朱德
Chungnan	Zhongnan	終南
Dabdar	Dabuda'er	達布達尔
Dali	Dali	大理
Dandan-ulik	Dandanwulike	丹丹烏里克
Dih	Dihe	迪和
Elossu	Eluosi	俄羅斯
Emin Hoja	Emin Hezhuo	額敏和卓

WADE-GILES	PINYIN	CHINESE
er-hu	erhu	二胡
Fa-hsien	Faxian	法顯
Famen	Famen	法門
Fu Hsi	Fu Xi	伏羲
Fufeng	Fufeng	扶風
Fukang	Fukang	阜康
Genghis Khan	Chengjisi Han	成吉思汗
Ghez	Gaizi	盖孜
gobi	gebi	戈壁
Hachi Hachip	Haji Hajifu	哈吉哈吉甫
Hami	Hami	哈密
Han (dynasty)	Han	漢
Hangchou	Hangzhou	杭州
Harbin	Ha'erbin	哈尔濱
Hochou	Hezhou	河州
Honan	Henan	河南

WADE-GILES	PINYIN	CHINESE
Hong Kong	Xianggang	香港
Hoping	Heping	和平
Hotien	Hetian	和田
Hsi-chun	Xijun	細君
Hsi-hsia	Xixia	西夏
Hsia (state)	Hsia	夏
hsiao	xiao	簫
Hsipo	Xibo	錫伯
Hsienyang	Xianyang	咸陽
Hsinchiang	Xinjiang	新疆
Hsing-hsing-hsia	Xingxingxia	星星峽
Hsiung-nu	Xiongnu	匈奴
Hsiwangmu	Xiwangmu	西王母
Hsiyouchi	Xiyouji	西遊記
Hsuan-tsang	Xuanzang	玄奘
Hsuan-tsung	Xuanzong	玄宗

WADE-GILES	PINYIN	CHINESE
Hui (ethnic group)	Hui	回
Huiyuan	Huiyuan	惠遠
Hungshan	Hongshan	紅山
Hungshanhsia	Hongshanxia	紅山峽
Huo Ch'u-ping	Huo Qubing	霍去病
Huochou	Huozhou	火州
Hupei	Hubei	湖北
Ili	Yili	伊犁
Iparhan	Yipa'erhan	伊帕尔汗
Junggar	Zhunge'er	準噶爾
Kai-ssu	Gaisi	盖斯
Kaifeng	Kaifeng	開封
Kanchou	Ganzhou	甘州
Kansu	Gansu	甘肅
Kao (emperor)	Gao	高
Kaochang	Gaochang	高昌

WADE-GILES	PINYIN	CHINESE
Karakorum	Kalakunlun	喀喇昆侖
karez	kanerjing	坎兒井
Karkul	Kalaku'er	卡拉庫尔
Kashgar	Kashi	喀什
Kazak	Hasake	哈薩克
khoja	huojia	霍加
Khotan	Hotian	和田
Kiangsu	Jiangsu	江蘇
Kirghiz	Ke'erkezi	柯尔克孜
Kizdorha	Kezi'erdoha	克孜尔朵哈
Kizil	Kezi'er	克孜尔
Kongur	Gongge'er	公格尔
Korgas	Huo'erguosi	霍尔果斯
Korla	Ku'erle	庫尔勒
kuan	guan	關
Kuangchou	Guangzhou	廣州

WADE-GILES	PINYIN	CHINESE
Kucha	Kuche	庫車
Kumarajiva	Jiumoluoshi	鳩摹羅什
kung-fu	gongfu	功夫
Kunjerab	Hongqilafu	紅其拉甫
Kunlun	Kunlun	崑崙
Lanchou	Lanzhou	蘭州
Lao-tzu	Laozi	老子
Lei Kung	Lei Gong	雷公
Li Kuang	Li Guang	李廣
Li Pai	Li Bai	李白
Liangchou	Liangzhou	涼州
Lichien	Lijian	驪軒
Lin Tse-hsu	Lin Zexu	林則徐
Linhsia	Linxia	臨夏
Lintung	Lintong	臨潼
Liuchiahsia	Liujiaxia	劉家峽

WADE-GILES	PINYIN	CHINESE
Liuyuan	Liyuan	柳園
Lo Wu	Luowu	羅湖
Lop	Luobu	羅布
Lop Nor	Luobu Nao'er	羅布淖尔
Loulan	Loulan	樓蘭
Lu (state, empress)	Lu	呂
Lu Kuang	Lu Guang	呂光
Lussu Tamu	Lusi Tamu	魯斯塔姆
Maichishan	Maijishan	麥積山
Manchu	Manzu	滿族
Mani	Moni	摹尼
Mao Tse-tung	Mao Zedong	毛澤東
Maoling	Maoling	茂陵
Melikwat	Mailike'awati	買利克阿瓦提
Meng T'ien	Meng Tian	蒙恬
Mingsha	Mingsha	鳴沙

WADE-GILES	PINYIN	CHINESE
Mintaka	Mingtiegai	明鐵蓋
Mohoyen	Moheyan	莫賀延
Mokao	Mogao	莫高
Molena Ashadin	Molina Ashading	莫里那 阿沙丁
Mongol	Menggu	蒙古
Mu (king)	Mu	穆
Muztagh-ata	Mushitage	慕士塔格
nan-hu	nanhu	南胡
nei-kung	neigong	內功
Ninghsia	Ningxia	寧夏
Nu-wa	Nuwa	女媧
Pai Chu-yi	Bai Juyi	白居易
Palikun	Bailikun	巴里坤
Pamir	Pami'er	帕米尔
Panhsi	Panxi	蟠溪
Paoan	Baoan	保安

WADE-GILES	PINYIN	CHINESE
Paochi	Baoji	寶鷄
P'an-ku	Pangu	盤古
Peishouling	Beishouling	北首嶺
Pientukou	Biandukou	扁都口
Pingling	Bingling	炳靈
p'i-p'a	pipa	琵琶
Pirali	Pilali	皮拉力
Polokenu	Poluokenu	婆羅科努
Salar	Sala	撒拉
Samu	Samu	薩姆
Sankuan	Sanguan	散關
Santaoling	Sandaoling	三道嶺
Sarikol	Seleku'er	色勒庫尔
Satuk	Satuke	薩圖克
Sha-liao-shu	Shaliaosuo	沙療所
Shantan	Shandan	山丹

WADE-GILES	PINYIN	CHINESE
shao-k'ao-jou	shao-kao-rou	燒烤肉
Shenchen	Shenzhen	深圳
Shensi	Shaanxi	陝西
Sian	Xi'an	西安
Ssu-ma Ch'ien	Sima Qian	司馬遷
Ssumen	Simen	絲門
Ssupao	Sibao	四堡
Subashi	Subashi	蘇巴什
Suchou	Suzhou	蘇州
Sui (dynasty)	Sui	隋
Sun Wu-k'ung	Sun Wukong	孫悟空
Sunan	Sunan	肅南
Sung (dynasty)	Song	宋
Szechuan	Sichuan	四川
Tahoyen	Daheyan	大河沿
Tajik	Tajike	塔吉克

Wade-Giles	Pinyin	Chinese
Taklamakan	Takelamagan	塔克拉瑪干
Tarim	Talimu	塔里木
Tamerlane	Tiemu'er	帖木兒
Tangho	Danghe	党河
Tao	Dao	道
Taoteching	Taodejing	道德經
Tarim	Talimu	塔里木
Tashkorgan	Tashiku'ergan	塔什庫尔干
Tatar	Tata'er	塔塔尔
Telemet	Telemite	特樂密特
Telig Timur	Tuheilu Tiemu'er	禿黑魯。帖木尔
Tengger	Tenggeli	騰格里
Tienchih	Tianchi	天池
Tienshan	Tianshan	天山
Tienshui	Tianshui	天水
Tingling	Dingling	丁零

Wade-Giles	Pinyin	Chinese
Tomur	Tuomu'er	托木尔
Topa	Tuoba	拓拔
Torgut	Tu'erhute	土尔扈特
Tung (tribe)	Dong	侗
Tunghsiang	Dongxiang	東鄉
Tunhuang	Dunhuang	敦煌
Turfan	Tulufan	吐魯番
t'ai-chi	taiji	太極
T'ang (dynasty)	Tang	唐
Uighur	Huige	回紇
Upar	Wupa'er	烏帕尔
Urumchi	Ulumuqi	烏魯木齊
Wa-fa	Wafa	瓦法
Wang Yuan-lu	Wang Yuanlu	王圓籙
Wei (dynasty)	Wei	魏
Wei (lady)	Wei	衛

WADE-GILES	PINYIN	CHINESE
Wei (river, village)	Wei	渭
Wen (king)	Wen	文
Wenshan	Wenshan	文山
Wu (emperor)	Wu	武
Wupao	Wubao	五堡
Wusun	Wusun	烏孫
Wutangshan	Wudangshan	武當山
Wuwei	Wuwei	武威
yang	yang	陽
Yang (emperor)	Yang	煬
Yang Kuei-fei	Yang Guifei	楊貴妃
yang-ch'in	yangqin	洋琴
Yangkuan	Yangguan	陽關
Yangshuo	Yangshuo	陽朔
Yangtze	Yangzi	揚子江
Yarnaz	Ya'ernaizi	牙尔乃孜

Wade-Giles	Pinyin	Chinese
Yengisar	Yingjisha	英吉沙
Yingchisha	Yingjisha	英吉沙
Yi-fu	Yifu	乙弗
Yiching	Yijing	易經
yin	yin	陰
Yining	Yining	伊寧
Yiwu	Yiwu	伊吾
Yotkan	Yutien	于闐
Yuku	Yugu	裕固
Yumen	Yumen	玉門
Yunnan	Yunnan	雲南
Yussup	Yusufu	玉素甫

Printed in the United States
by Baker & Taylor Publisher Services